YESTERDAY'S

HEROES

YESTERDAY'S

HEROES

National Hunt Edition

GRAHAM BUDDRY

Matador
9 Priory Business Park
Kibworth Beauchamp
Leicester LE8 0RX, UK
Tel: (+44) 116 279 2299
Fax: (+44) 116 279 2277
Email: books@troubador.co.uk
Web: www.troubador.co.uk/matador

ISBN 978 1780880 068

British Library Cataloguing in Publication Data.
A catalogue record for this book is available from the British Library.

Typeset in 11pt Book Antiqua by Troubador Publishing Ltd, Leicester, UK
Printed and bound in the UK by TJ International, Padstow, Cornwall

Matador is an imprint of Troubador Publishing Ltd

This book is dedicated to all the horses, great and not so great, who have provided endless enjoyment to myself and millions of others down the years.

CONTENTS

FOREWORD

There can be few greater spectacles in the sporting world than the racehorse. Whether this is a Supreme Champion exerting his authority with spine tingling brilliance or two Gladiators battling it out in a race where neither will give in until the crowds are cheering them both in the same breath.

This book does not pretend to be a definitive list of the best over the years as some Goliaths of the racing world have not been included in this edition while other entrants may be lesser known to the reader. What is certain is that each was a Hero in his own way.

Some of the chapters cover an entire career while concentrating on a defining event while others highlight just a single race. In these, although there may be a few exceptions, most have never been presented in this way before.

In each I have attempted to bring something new to the reader, often in the angle I am portraying the race, once even from the horse's point of view, and I hope you'll forgive me this indulgence.

I have learnt many new things about the old friends depicted in these pages and I hope you enjoy this book as much as I enjoyed writing it.

ONE MAN

The British are a strange people. They love a hero but they also love to see a hero brought down to earth. Finally they love to see a once-great rise up and attain the impossible one last time. In equine terms no horse comes closer to this than One Man.

Foaled on 24 May 1988, the grey son of top flat performer, Remainder Man, was to achieve the heights in performing a unique double and show an Achilles heel like no other before taking race fans to the pinnacle of both ecstasy and despair in the space of 17 days.

As a novice hurdler in the 1992/93 season One Man was nothing out of the ordinary, winning three modest races from 9 starts. Ominously his worst race came at Cheltenham where he finished 30 lengths behind the winner. The following season the Gordon Richards trained gelding was sent novice chasing and a glimmer of the brilliance to come started to show through.

The second of five consecutive victories was achieved at Haydock Park where One Man gave three pounds and a ten length thrashing to the very capable Monsieur Le Cure. At the Cheltenham Festival that season the unbeaten One Man was well fancied in the Sun Alliance Novice Chase and while old adversary Monsieur Le Cure won nicely, One Man showed his loathing for Cheltenham again by finishing 49 lengths behind the winner.

The following season One Man ran only four times, winning a three runner affair at Ayr before heading to Newbury to win the Hennessy Cognac Gold Cup under the feather weight of just 10 stone. After this he failed to complete in his other two races, a minor injury at Kempton Park curtailing his season.

Back as a seven year old, One Man started his campaign by giving a seven length beating to Jodami, albeit getting over a stone before winning again at the expense of Monsieur Le Cure.

Atrocious weather ruled out Kempton's Christmas showpiece but the King George VI chase was re-scheduled for Sandown Park on the 6th of January. By this time many were doubting One Man's ability to really see out a three mile trip and while Kempton Park may not have stretched any suspect stamina, Sandown's stiffer track and uphill finish certainly would. In the end it made no difference as One Man ran brilliantly to put 14 lengths between himself and the runner-up, Monsieur Le Cure.

And so to Cheltenham again, this time for the Gold Cup itself. Until two fences from home there was really only one winner but One Man stopped as if shot soon afterwards and was out on his feet as he struggled to the line in 6th place, some 34 lengths behind Imperial Call.

The 1996/97 season began with One Man dishing out a seven length beating to Barton Bank before storming home in the King George, back at Kempton on Boxing day, by an incredibly easy 12 lengths. In so doing, One Man had performed a unique double in winning the same annual contest twice in one year. Now One Man was definitely at the top of the racing tree and a force to be reckoned with.

Gordon Richards and owner, John Hales, then decided to try and lay the Cheltenham jinx by running One Man back at the course in the Pillar Properties chase at the end of January. In a thrilling race One Man stayed on up the hill and battled for all his worth to deny Barton Bank by a head...surely all this nonsense about One Man and Cheltenham would now cease.

After a prep race at Ascot where Strong Promise proved to be a length too good over a seemingly inadequate trip, One Man lined up again in the Gold Cup. In a replay of the previous year there was again only one obvious winner until they turned into the home straight for the final time when One Man again hit the wall. Thirty five weary lengths separated the 6th placed One Man from Mr Mulligan as critics laid into One Man, a one-time hero who stopped on the Cheltenham hill like no other horse in living memory. To compound his season, One Man went to Aintree and ran no race at all before being pulled up behind Barton Bank.

One Man's final season started at Wetherby with his third victory over Barton Bank before moving on to the Peterborough chase at Huntingdon at the end of November. In this 2½ mile contest, One Man dished out a nine length beating to the super tough Viking Flagship. Back at Kempton Park for the King George, One Man and Richard Dunwoody tried to win for the third time but, even though only rising ten, One Man looked an old horse as he finished an exceptionally long way behind See More Business.

The same supposedly inadequate trip at Ascot was again chosen as One Man's Cheltenham prep race and this time he surprised everyone by beating Strong Promise quite comfortably.

As the Cheltenham Festival approached again, Gordon Richards made the bold statement that due to the experiences of the previous two years, One Man would not contest the Gold Cup. Instead he would be aimed at the 2 mile Queen Mother Champion Chase. In many circles this was looked upon with raised eyebrows as One Man had never won over the distance; indeed he had only run over the minimum trip once in his life when way down the field on his racecourse debut 6 years earlier.

And so, on the 18th March 1998, One Man lined up at his dreaded Cheltenham for what was to be the final time. With Tony Dobbin injured, Brian Harding, who was yet to ride a Festival winner, took the reins for the first time.

The field of eight was headed by the giant 9 year old, Ask Tom, the 5/2 favourite after two recent victories. Former winner Klairon Davis started at 100/30 while One Man was bracketed on 7/2 with the Martin Pipe trained, Or Royal. Another previous winner, Viking Flagship started at 9/1 and the gallant 11 year old would be retired after this race while the other three runners were unconsidered in the betting.

The race was run at a cracking pace with Russ Garritty on Ask Tom vying for the lead with One Man while Klairon Davis, Viking Flagship, outsider Lord Dorcet and Or Royal followed in their wake a few lengths adrift. Ask Tom was jumping superbly and out jumped One Man to briefly go half a length up, then One Man pulled half a length clear but Ask Tom was soon back with him as they tried to stretch the field. Heading down the hill to three out and Ask Tom came under pressure while One Man was still hard held, Klairon Davis starting to be nudged along in third place while Or Royal closed down on Lord Dorcet, Viking Flagship valiantly running on at one pace. Three out and One Man flew it a length to the good, Ask Tom under strong driving from Lord Dorcet and Or Royal getting into the picture. Two out and the cheers started to go up for One Man as the rest of the field looked held. The final fence and One Man took it well, daylight between him and his pursuers as Ask Tom faded, the crowd cheering wildly as One Man came up the dreaded hill in front, starting to tire a little but a comfortable 4 lengths to spare over Tony McCoy on Or Royal and Lord Dorcet, Klairon Davis staying on into fourth place just ahead of Viking Flagship and the exhausted Ask Tom.

Cheered to the echo as finally he strode into the hallowed winners enclosure, One Man had done it at last. Racegoers openly wept as he received a rapturous reception, his name now forever on the roll of honour. Perhaps he should have run in this race before but it seemed certain that he would run in it again, defending his crown and maybe proving to be one of the truly greats over 2 miles.

Seventeen days later Brian Harding took the ride again as One Man went to Aintree, fully expected to crown his wonderful season with a final victory. Running and jumping well One Man was clearly enjoying himself when he met a fence all wrong, crashed through it and fell in a heap on the far side, his shoulder broken.

Nobody cared any more about the race up front…all eyes were turned to the stricken One Man as a hush fell over the racecourse, only the race tannoy breaking the deathly silence. Binoculars quivered as the dreaded green screens were erected, tears running freely down many a face. Seventeen short days ago the tears were for unbridled happiness and now they were for the grief of a champion. The green screens came down and One Man, Hennessy winner, dual King George winner, Champion Chaser and holder of all our hearts was gone for ever.

SEA PIGEON

There's an old adage in racing that you should bet with your head and not with your heart, but on those rare occasions when the heart rules and a nation's favourite racehorse wins, well, it's a very special moment indeed.

Cheltenham's Champion Hurdle of 1980 was one such race.

Nine runners went to post for a record prize of £24,972 for which the mighty Monksfield started as the 6/5 favourite. Monksfield, one of the toughest horses of all was the reigning dual Champion Hurdler and after a series of below par performances earlier in the season had burst back to form with a gallant one length second in the Erin Foods Champion Hurdle at Leopardstown 3 weeks earlier. Giving nine pounds to the winning favourite he led one hurdle out and ran on gamely to go under by just one length. Whichever way you looked at it, the Champion, who always produced his best efforts at Cheltenham, was back.

Connaught Ranger had won the Erin Foods Champion Hurdle the previous season and hadn't been out of the frame in six races this season, twice finishing ahead of Bird's Nest, once when conceding four pounds, before finishing behind the same horse on their last run before Cheltenham. Connaught Ranger, an ultra consistent sort, would start at 12/1 for the Championship.

Bird's Nest had distinguished himself in the last four Champion Hurdles, finishing second to Night Nurse in 1976 with previous winners Comedy of Errors and Lanzarote behind him and started favourite for the race the following year. The real "plus" to his name was in Newcastle's Fighting Fifth hurdle on 17th November when he was headed at the last by Sea Pigeon but rallied so gamely that he won by 1½ lengths, even though he was conceding eight pounds to the runner up.

After this he was awarded the valuable Christmas hurdle at Kempton on the controversial disqualification of Celtic Ryde after a driving finish had left only a short head between the pair. With 3 wins from 5 starts and Sea Pigeon clearly held on form, the 11/1 on offer looked generous.

Sea Pigeon was the people's champion. By the magnificent Sea Bird II, he had run seventh in the Derby as a three year old and although he was a brilliant hurdler, many doubted he would ever be crowned champion. This would be his fourth attempt at the race in which he had been runner up to Monksfield in both the previous years. Last year he had looked to be cantering all over his main adversary as they rounded the final bend into the straight, but while Monksfield battled every inch to the line, Sea Pigeon fought as best he could but couldn't maintain the momentum and there seemed no real reason why this year should be very different. Indeed the two had met on five separate occasions and Monksfield had finished ahead of Sea Pigeon every time. Before his Fighting Fifth defeat at Newcastle, Sea Pigeon had started his campaign with a fall in a four horse race when going as easily as a hard odds on shot should be. The horse that finished second that day, Capers Lad, was then easily trounced by 12 lengths in a two horse affair at Sandown where no SP was returned. Connaught Ranger had previously beaten the same horse by an equally easy 13½ lengths when conceding him one pound more than Sea Pigeon had. When you consider that only a week before Cheltenham he was a doubtful runner with a poisoned foot it is easy to see that "heart" money was all that was supporting him at 13/2 in the betting market.

Pollardstown, at 5 years old, was representing the younger brigade. He had won the Triumph Hurdle the previous season and was a red hot favourite in his latest race at Wincanton where he was cruising in the lead despite some poor jumping when he fell at the last flight. Prior to that he had gotten up close home to beat Connaught Ranger by 2½ lengths at Sandown after having fallen on his seasonal debut at Ascot. At 7/2, only Monksfield was preferred in the betting.

Of the other runners, Paiute a 22/1 shot had won two of his three races as well as winning the French Champion Hurdle the previous season. Broadleas, at 25/1 had his preferred soft ground and had won his last three races against modest opposition. Royal Boxer was a 300/1 outsider, while Norfolk Dance at 25/1 was another who would relish the soft ground. Having run at distances up to 3 miles with some very difficult tasks at the weights, Norfolk Dance had still won twice, most recently beating the odds on Celtic Ryde at level weights over 2½ miles at Cheltenham in January. This was Celtic Ryde's first real defeat of the season and although not in the race himself, the form would give Norfolk Dance at least the semblance of a chance.

As far as Sea Pigeon was concerned, the only thing in his favour was the recent change to the course which would mean running a furlong less than in previous years, but no horse in the history of the race had ever won his first Champion Hurdle as a ten year old. With the sole exception of Hatton's Grace who won in 1949 as a nine year old and then repeated the feat in 1950 and 1951, only one horse aged in double figures had even made the frame and that was when the ten year old Another Flash was second, way back in 1964.

From the start, Paiute, the French Champion led the field until making a mistake at the fourth where Monksfield took over as they charged down the hill with Pollardstown, Bird's Nest and Connaught Ranger in hot pursuit and tracking these with ominous ease was Sea Pigeon. Norfolk Dance and Broadleas were hopelessly outclassed and Royal Boxer was never in with a chance until running on through beaten horses to take a career high fourth place.

At the business end of the race Monksfield swung into the straight, the reigning champion on his favourite track. Pollardstown and Connaught Ranger now found the difference between being very good and being great and try as they might they couldn't stay with the pace of the leaders. Bird's Nest was running his usual gallant race but he, too, was flat to the boards and making no impression on Monksfield.

Hugging the rail and moving up on that final turn was the black figure of Sea Pigeon, swinging along with apparent ease, in direct contrast to the hard driving of Monksfield just ahead of him.

Monksfield and Sea Pigeon flew the last in an exact replay of the previous two years, but there the similarity ended. In the past Monksfield had fought and fought again to deny the flying Pigeon but this time, while Monksfield was giving his customary all, Sea Pigeon, incredibly, was about to re-write Champion Hurdle history. Monksfield, hard under the whip stayed on with his customary guts but Sea Pigeon, with Jonjo O'Neill riding out with just hands and heels, simply changed gear and started to draw clear. In the grandstands thousands of cheering voices realised that fairytales really do come true and to a fantastic chorus, Sea Pigeon surged clear to win by seven lengths from Monksfield with Bird's Nest another 1½ lengths back in third place.

In a golden age of hurdling superstars, Sea Pigeon was probably not the best of them all but without doubt he was the most popular and this victory brought a lump to the throat of many hardened racegoers.

At an age when most people thought his best years were behind him, Sea Pigeon had claimed the crown. Incredibly, the following year Sea Pigeon and Bird's Nest contested the Champion Hurdle again and this time John Francome, deputising for the injured Jonjo O'Neill, waited incredibly late, well after the last hurdle, before releasing Sea Pigeon's devastating final burst of speed to beat Pollardstown and with the cheers ringing to the echo, become a dual Champion Hurdler at the age of eleven to ensure his place among the immortals.

SILVER BUCK

Every once in a while a racehorse comes along which is so immeasurably superior to his contempories that it's simply frightening.

After the exploits of first Golden Miller and then Arkle we waited another generation before the brilliant, but forever nervous, head of Silver Buck graced racecourses wherever he went.

Such was his prowess that he scared away all but a handful of the opposition on more than 20 occasions throughout his illustrious career. On five separate occasions the handicapper tried to steady him with the mammoth weight of 12 stone 7 pounds, once with 12-6 and once with 12-3 and it's to Silver Buck's credit that he won all bar one of those races, the only blemish being when he finished a one length runner up when trying to give nearly two and a half stone to a horse that would go on to finish 3rd in a Cheltenham Gold Cup!

Injuries and illnesses which resulted in a lack of fitness at crucial times are the sole reasons why Silver Buck didn't win more than the single Cheltenham Gold Cup and pair of King George VI steeplechases in his glittering career.

As eternal proof of his undoubted brilliance, let's turn the clock back to November 24th 1982 at Haydock Park for the Edward Hanmer memorial Trophy.

Silver Buck, despite the steadier of 12 stone on his back was the firm 8/11 favourite in a select field of 5.

In his previous race, Silver Buck had made all to win unchallenged by a distance from the smart Gambling Prince and prior to that had won the Terry Biddlecombe chase at Wincanton by an easy 7 lengths.

Silver Buck had farmed this particular race in each of the three preceding seasons, winning comfortably for the first time back in 1979 from Night Nurse. The following year he gave the ten year old Royal

Mail 9 pounds and a 13 lengths beating…not bad when you consider that Royal Mail had finished 2nd in the 1979 Gold Cup. On to 1981 and Night Nurse was back in third place this time, beaten by more than 30 lengths, with Sunset Cristo receiving nearly a stone when 1½ lengths runner up.

Today the 6/1 shot, Sunset Cristo, would be receiving a stone and two pounds in his quest to improve on his Gold Cup 3rd place to Silver Buck the previous season. On his only run of the season so far, Sunset Cristo had finished third to Bregawn, the horse who only a few months later would be heading Michael Dickinson's famous five in this season's Cheltenham Gold Cup.

Royal Judgement was readily available at 8/1 as this top class chaser was getting only six pounds from the star attraction. His two runs already this season had seen Royal Judgement giving away huge lumps of weight when 3rd as favourite at Ascot and before that when 4th as favourite in the Charisma Chase at Kempton when trying to give over a stone to the winner and two stone to the 2nd and 3rd placed horses.

Later in the season, Royal Judgement would be top weight for the Welsh Grand National, finish second to Observe in the Gainsborough chase at Sandown when conceding 5 pounds for a 2 length defeat with previous Gold Cup winner, Little Owl, back in 3rd place. Among other top class form he would be the top weighted favourite for the Irish Grand National and then finish 3rd in the Whitbread after cruising into the lead 3 out before finding his welter burder too much against two lightly weighted opponents.

The next of the days runners was the former Cheltenham Gold Cup winner, Master Smudge. Although still only a ten year old, the same age as Silver Buck, and receiving 21 pounds in weight he was freely available at 25/1. In his four races so far, Master Smudge had been anchored by enormous weights, his best efforts being to win under 12-7 at Taunton and lumping 12-5 into second place after leading at halfway and being clear 5 out before the 10 stone bottom weight headed him approaching the last fence at Stratford.

On paper at least, Sunset Cristo, Royal Judgement and Master Smudge could be said to have at least a fighting chance, but it was the other runner which the bookies priced at 3/1 second favourite for the race.

Jenny Pitman had never been a trainer to play down her horses and here she had a star in the making and fully expected him "to give Silver Buck one hell of a fright".

Indeed, having started his season at Stratford by cantering all over his rivals to lead very easily at the last fence, he followed this up at Ascot in the Lambert and Butler Premier Chase qualifier where, as the 6/4 favourite, he won easily by 25 lengths.

The following season Burrough Hill Lad would sweep all before him in the Welsh Grand National, Gainsborough Chase and Cheltenham Gold Cup before going on to further glory in the Hennesey Gold Cup and King George VI Chase, but today he was the rising star against the established champion and the massive one and a half stone advantage he had in weight made Silver Buck's task, in hindsight, look formidable indeed.

At the off Sunset Cristo tried to keep company with Silver Buck until he blundered badly 5 fences from home, while Royal Judgement was always prominent until coming under pressure 3 out where he faded out of contention.

Master Smudge had soon lost touch which just left Burrough Hill Lad, who had made a few mistakes with his jumping early on, to track Silver Buck into the home straight.

Silver Buck was giving his rivals a lesson in clean, swift jumping, meeting every fence spot on and as they cleared the third last fence he was still going with ominous ease from Burrough Hill Lad who, in receipt of all that weight, still looked to have every chance.

Silver Buck was well known to idle when he hit the front and Burrough Hill Lad was a doughty battler but the race was decided in spectacular fashion as they cleared the last fence together. In a matter of a few strides, Silver Buck had powered 3 lengths clear before starting to idle in his customary way, maintaining the margin to the line.

Depending which form book you read the result is the same but the 'close up' has different words: Burrough Hill Lad was "murdered for foot after the last" or "Silver Buck gave away the weight and paralysed Burrough Hill Lad".

After the race Michael Dickinson, Silver Buck's trainer, knowing how much was expected of Burrough Hill Lad, had a quiet chat with his formidable trainer, Jenny Pitman.

He said; "I've had a word with Silver Buck and he told me that he hadn't been at all afraid of Burrough Hill Lad. But I'll tell you what, Jenny, I'm frightened to death of you."

She replied: "You're not, are you Dicky?"

"Yes I am - most men are, aren't they Jenny?"

Whichever way you look at it Burrough Hill Lad was an extremely good horse but Silver Buck was one of the greatest horses ever to grace the turf. Haydock Park was his favourite track and on form such as this, even Arkle would have been playing for second place.

YAHOO: THOUGHTS OF A RACEHORSE

My name is Yahoo and I am, or were, a racehorse. Some would probably say not a very good racehorse and they may be right but in the space of just a few weeks in my entire career I would become famous.

It's not that I actually won a race that made me famous but that I was beaten. In fact, in coming second I will be remembered forever.

On the morning of Thursday 16th March 1989 I woke to a wonderful sight. As I peered over my stable door there was snow everywhere that it hadn't already turned to slush. For me, as a professional racehorse, this was great as it meant the ground for my race that afternoon would be heavy, so I would have a chance that I wouldn't normally have had. Importantly, though, it would act against some of the other aspirants.

My race was the Cheltenham Gold Cup, the most important race of the year and the target for all the best horses in training. I knew a lot about most of the other runners I would be racing against and it really was a high class turnout, but some were far better than the rest of us.

A former Gold Cup Winner, The Thinker, with two wins from just three races this season, had a lot of support and would love the ground, as would the reigning Champion, Charter Party. Last years runner-up, Cavvies Clown, would be trying again as well, along with the high class, but doubtful stayer, Pegwell Bay.

Not short of stamina would be the former Grand National winner, West Tip, nor Welsh National winner, Bonanza Boy, who had won three of his four races this season, although everyone considered the race to be between just three other runners, and I wasn't considered to be one of them.

Over from Ireland was the 7 year old monster called Carvill's Hill. I'd heard he was something extra special and would simply love the wet ground and had already won three of his four races this season as well, but could sometimes be a bit chancy at his fences. With his huge reputation it seemed that if he stood up he must win.

From England was another potential superstar called Ten Plus who had won four races from five starts this season but was another who would sometimes hit a fence very hard. I'd heard that a year or so ago he'd had an exceptionally bad fall at Cheltenham and it really knocked his confidence for a long time.

With just those two against the rest of us it would be a good race but a so-called living legend would be in the race as well. His name was Desert Orchid, popularly known as Dessie.

I hadn't raced against him before but those who had had said he was by far the best horse they had ever seen and would fight for ever and never knew when to give up. The other things I knew were that he wouldn't like the ground, had never won going left handed and simply hated Cheltenham, having lost every time he'd run here. Today we'd see just how good he could be.

I was really super fit and thought I had a great chance with only Carvill's Hill and Ten Plus to worry about. I couldn't really see The Thinker, Charter Party or the others getting away from me and everything seemed stacked against Desert Orchid. All being well I'd have a great race.

How clearly I remember that day! Walking around the parade ring waiting for my jockey then the parade in front of the stands before cantering to the start. How awful that ground was - what joy for us mud larks - then circling round at the start.

We're being called in... *"The thirteen runners are under starters' orders. Captain Michael Sayers is about to start his last Gold Cup."*

I've got a good position on the tape - must stay handy - you can't win this race from too far back.

"They're away and to a great roar from the crowd they race to the first of the 22 fences."

I'm away well, Desert Orchid is on my left. Up and over the first. This ground is really wet and muddy...now the next fence.

Desert Orchid leads as I knew he would, Charter Party next with Bonanza Boy and Ten Plus then me. I've got the position I wanted. Past the stands and round the turn in 5th place, nice and wide to get a good look at these fences, these tough fences, the water jump, first of the ditches then another plain one...sounds like someone fell there.

"It looks like Golden Freeze has gone at that one."

Another ditch. Behind to my left I think another one fell.

"Carvill's Hill has gone there."

'Carvill's Hill is down' call a few of the others. Unlucky for him but a better chance for the rest of us.

"The hope of Ireland has gone at the second ditch."

Another fence then starting to run downhill – a bit of a breather – Desert Orchid still in the lead from Charter Party and Pegwell Bay, Ten Plus and myself, still wide, still up there, still going well.

Now the 10th, this tricky downhill fence.

"And The Thinker's gone at that one!"

Another mud lark, another real danger is out.

"Ten left now in the 1989 Gold Cup."

Two more in the straight and it's still Desert Orchid, Ten Plus, Charter Party and myself. Cavvies Clown sprinting through on my outside – doesn't he know we've got to go round again?

Round the turn and downhill, ten left to jump and that big horse, Ten Plus, has gone to the front. Desert Orchid has the rail. Bonanza Boy has moved up on the outside with Slalom then Charter Party and Cavvies Clown – I must keep my place with them – I'm 7th now ... this is where the race really starts.

"Racing now to the final ditch, six from home and Ten Plus has taken a 3 length advantage from Desert Orchid. Charter Party, the former winner, is third."

I'm up to 4th again, just ahead of Cavvies Clown and Pegwell Bay.

"Beautiful jump by Desert Orchid takes him to within a length of Ten Plus..."

Top of the hill now and Ten Plus leads by 3 lengths again but he's being pushed along. Desert Orchid is next but he hates the ground and the course. I'm running next with Charter Party. I still feel good and seem to be going best of all.

"Four to jump now with Ten Plus with a 4 length advantage over Desert

Orchid, still in there fighting, Yahoo coming there, he loves the mud, on the far side, Charter Party is fourth."

Ten Plus still leads but he's being pushed along hard, Desert Orchid is tracking him, I'm going so easily, then Charter Party…we've got the race between us. Now downhill to that dreaded third last fence.

Ten Plus is driven into it – he's fallen – hell, that was a bad fall…I hope he'll be alright.

"Ten Plus has gone! He's left Desert Orchid in the lead. It's Desert Orchid now as they race to the home turn, Yahoo chasing him all the time and trying to get up on the inside with Charter Party third."

He's left a gap on the rails! I'm still going well and cruise into the gap for the home turn. Desert Orchid is being pushed along and I can hear Charter Party under strong driving behind. The Cheltenham Gold Cup and I'm going to win it! I've only got to see off Desert Orchid now…the living legend…yeah, right!

"Desert Orchid and Yahoo now as they race round the home turn, there's very little between them, Yahoo on the far side, he's gone on now, from Desert Orchid towards the near side."

This is it. Now I go and win the race.

"Yahoo from Desert Orchid and Desert Orchid looks as though he's tiring in the ground, Yahoo, who loves the mud, is full of running at the second last."

Measure it, steady, meet it right, up and over, a good jump, still going well and half a length up…won't he ever go away?

"Yahoo jumps from Desert Orchid, but Desert Orchid is rallying, he's trying to come again."

I can't shake him off. I'm going well enough but he's really tough. We'll see about that after the last when I go for home. Charter Party isn't too far away either – he's run a great race but won't catch me now.

"Desert Orchid's accelerating as they come to the last, Yahoo on the far side, Desert Orchid on the near side."

Over the last and neither of us jump it that well. I'm only a length up but this hill is tough. I've got to give everything I've got now but he still won't go away.

"Desert Orchid on the near side, Yahoo on the far side. Desert Orchid is drifting over towards the far side."

What the…? He's nearly level but he's coming to get me, he's coming right at me…what sort of monster is he?

I'm trying as hard as I can but he's still there, he's nearly on top of me! Pull him away from me…pull him away!

"He's beginning to get up…Desert Orchid is beginning to get up!"

I've done my best. More than my best. I can't give any more.

"As they race towards the line there's a tremendous cheer from the crowd as Desert Orchid is gonna win it – Desert Orchid has won the Gold Cup! Yahoo is second, third is Charter Party…"

He's stopped, exhausted, after the line. I join him - well done - Charter Party soon joins us, he's given his all as well.

"Dessie has done it. Desert Orchid has won it!"

Doesn't like the ground, doesn't like running left handed, doesn't like Cheltenham!? The only thing I know for sure is that I tried my best. I still have some energy left but I couldn't go any faster. Not against a living legend. Not against Desert Orchid.

"You've never heard cheers like this at Cheltenham…the crowd is going absolutely wild…Desert Orchid, the 5/2 favourite – everybody's favourite."

A few weeks later I raced Desert Orchid and Charter Party again at Aintree. It was a cracking race and history will show that my Cheltenham run was no fluke for although both Desert Orchid and Charter Party both fell, I was unbeatable that day and recorded the biggest win of my career.

Be that as it may, it was for a defeat I will always be remembered as it takes two to make a race. The legendary Desert Orchid and Yahoo, as together we conspired to produce arguably the greatest race of all time!

JAIR DU COCHET

Steeplechasing and Steeplechasers are so quintessentially the domain of the English and Irish that the mere thought of Johnny Foreigner being clever enough to train a horse, or indeed even having an animal good enough to compete with even the most modest of ours had always seemed laughable.

Some years ago a French trainer, virtually unknown in these shores, sent a lump of a horse to compete against our established stars in no less a race than the King George VI Chase at Kempton.

Uncared about and generally unbacked it was a major shock to the establishment when superstars such as Desert Orchid and Forgive 'n' Forget were firmly put in their place by Nupsala. In many quarters it seemed that racing had been brought into disrepute by such a result.

Over the following years Francois Doumen continued to plunder some of our top races with the likes of King George winners, Algan and First Gold, dual World hurdle winner, Barracouda, and The Fellow who not only won the King George twice but won the Cheltenham Gold Cup and was only inches away from winning it on two other occasions as well. Doumen himself won the universal respect of the National Hunt world and in many ways was considered an honorary Englishman.

Michael Dickinson and to a greater extent Martin Pipe, followed in later years by Paul Nicholls, are perhaps the best known trainers who quickly realised that some excellent types could be garnered from the French. As a result British racing has benefited from the influx of horses from Sabin Du Loir to Azertyuiop and Kauto Star to name just a very select few.

Despite these ongoing lessons there were a few raised eyebrows when another relatively unknown French trainer called Guillamme Macaire brought his stable star, Jair Du Cochet to England to take on the near invincible Best Mate in Huntingdon's biggest race of the season, the Peterborough Chase on the 22nd November 2003.

Henrietta Knight had farmed this race over the preceding years with Edredon Bleu winning four years running and then Best Mate himself 12 months ago.

Although lightly campaigned it was nearly two years since Best Mate had last been beaten and then he had been a gallant second to Florida Pearl in the King George VI Chase at Kempton. Since then he had won the Cheltenham Gold Cup twice and was backed into 8/13 for this, his seasonal debut in the field of six.

The Paul Nicholls trained Valley Henry had been fourth in the Gold Cup in March and had been going well enough when falling in his only run this season in the Charlie Hall Chase and some shrewd punters helped themselves to the 7/1 on offer.

Another seasonal debutant at 9/1 was La Landiere, another French bred, who had won her last seven chases at distances between 2 miles and 2 miles 5 furlongs, which included the prestigious Cathcart Chase at the Cheltenham Festival.

Rank outsiders Strong Magic, the third Irish bred horse in the field, and Venn Ottery, the sole English representative had no chance on paper and that was how it would transpire in the race with them both failing to trouble the principals.

The exceptionally good looking, near black gelding, Jair Du Cochet was well supported at 100/30 and it was easy to see why when you looked back through his form.

As a juvenile hurdler, Jair Du Cochet proved virtually unbeatable and it seems that only the foot-and-mouth outbreak denied him victory in the Triumph hurdle. The Racing Post said of him: "Probably the best juvenile hurdler seen in Britain in decades".

The following season he didn't quite live up to expectations against seasoned staying hurdlers, but that mattered little as his future clearly lay over fences where, as a novice, he rattled up an unbeaten four impressive victories, culminating in the Feltham Novice Chase at Kempton on Boxing day.

Next up was the Reynoldstown Chase at Ascot where Jair Du Cochet unseated his jockey, Jacques Ricou, at the final ditch when he and Keen Leader were well clear of the rest of the field.

Ricou had come in for some criticism of his tactics and moderate jockeyship on several occasions before Ascot, but he was virtually crucified for his ride at the Cheltenham Festival. In the Sun Alliance Novice Chase, the Gold Cup for novices, Ricou held Jair Du Cochet up too far in the rear and still hadn't moved a muscle at the top of the hill for the final time. To most observers, Jair Du Cochet, was easily going the best of all as he quickly improved into third place three out and was then, inexplicably, left to idle while they turned for home. He was still cruising when he pecked at the last and only then did Ricou go ineffectively for the whip in a manner which left many punters furious. The bare facts will record that One Knight won by 1¾ lengths from Jair Du Cochet and that is due entirely to such an awful ride by Ricou.

The next season started with Jair Du Cochet running twice over hurdles in France before lining up against Best Mate and company at Huntingdon.

As the starter sent the field on their way it was La Landiere who sped to the front but was out jumped by Jair Du Cochet who then took up the running over the next four fences. Best Mate, giving five pounds to his main rival, took a keen early hold and raced just in behind with La Landiere with Valley Henry tracking these.

At the 5th fence Best Mate took it up and started to stretch the field out a little but at the 9th Jair Du Cochet regained the lead with another extravagant leap. This was clearly two top class chasers, fully fit and well and at the top of their game. Valley Henry and La Landiere tried to stay with the two leaders while Strong Magic and Venn Ottery started to drop away as Jair Du Cochet quickened the pace again.

Best Mate was starting to be niggled along by his jockey, Jim Culloty, before making a mistake four out while Jair Du Cochet looked every bit a champion at the head of affairs. Three out and Valley Henry made a mistake while La Landiere started to weaken badly, Jair Du Cochet was still cantering with Best Mate trying his utmost a few lengths adrift and then being seriously shaken up as they approached the penultimate fence. Here Valley Henry was being ridden hard and began dropping away while La Landiere blundered badly and started to tail off.

With just one fence left to jump Jair Du Cochet was clear, he only had to jump it to win. Best Mate was staying on at one pace with Valley Henry a couple of lengths further back. Jair Du Cochet was not going to meet the last right though, Ricou again was indecisive as his mount ran badly left down the fence before hitting it hard. To gasps from the stands, Ricou, managed to stay in the saddle and, once balanced again, Jair Du Cochet ran on well to score an emphatic 8 length victory over Best Mate and Valley Henry.

For such a handsome and talented horse the chasing world seemed to lay at his feet yet this six year old would only race twice more.

As the 2/1 favourite for the King George at Kempton, Ricou again anchored Jair Du Cochet at the rear of the field where a modest mistake at only the fourth fence all but unseated the hapless jockey. Horse and rider continued uncomfortably for another mile before being pulled up amid a lot of head shaking at Macaire's continued use of a jockey who was not exactly in the top echelons of his trade.

At Cheltenham in January Jair Du Cochet ran in the Pillar Property Chase, a recognised Gold Cup trial and his last race before the big one in March. Under a more enterprising ride from Ricou, the 11/4 shot ran well throughout to score a decisive 12 length victory from Rince Ri. Favourite for that race was Therealbandit who fell four out just as he was starting to race, although it is highly doubtful if he would have beaten the winner. The previous seasons Gold Cup runner up, Truckers Tavern, unseated three out when well behind while Valley Henry and Sir Rembrandt were both pulled up when well beaten.

With the Cheltenham Gold Cup beckoning and a mouth-watering future to look forward to, Guillaume Macaire was putting the finishing touches to his stable star in France when tragedy happened. Jair Du Cochet was cantering in his normal work as he had many times before when his leg just broke. Nothing could be done and with Cheltenham on the horizon, Jair Du Cochet was put down.

A few weeks later Best Mate won the race for a third time, beating Sir Rembrandt into second place with Therealbandit and Valley Henry further down the field. On known form, that beautiful black horse would have gone very close to winning.

So the next time some upstart from the Continent dares to challenge English and Irish supremacy at the sport we love so well, think of Nupsala and Algan, Barracouda, The Fellow and First Gold and don't write them off too soon.

Most of all think of Jair Du Cochet. Not just of what might have been, but that glorious day at Huntingdon when he showed exactly what he could do against the very best we had to offer.

BURROUGH HILL LAD

On Boxing day, 1984, a huge crowd gathered at Kempton Park racecourse to witness what was to prove one of the finest runnings of the 3 mile, King George VI steeplechase in many years.

There were only three runners in the race, second only to the Cheltenham Gold Cup in importance, but they represented the highest possible class.

Burrough Hill Lad, the 1-2 favourite, was fully expected to add this valuable prize to the Hennessey Cognac Gold Cup he had won impressively at Newbury exactly one month earlier under the burden of 12 stone, the Cheltenham Gold Cup itself from the previous March and a massive total of £138,000 already won in prize money.

His main adversary on this bright, crisp afternoon, with a prize money record of £166,000 was Wayward Lad, winner of this prestigious event in each of the last two seasons. Also in his favour was the fact that Wayward Lad always produced his best around the tight Sunbury circuit, whereas Burrough Hill Lad had yet to win on the course. As such, Wayward Lad was a very well supported 5-2 in the betting market.

The 13-2 outsider of the three runners was Combs Ditch, who was having his first steeplechase and only his second race in 20 months following an internal haemorrhage and breathing problems when finishing a very distressed second favourite in the 1982 Cheltenham Gold Cup.

All three participants had had their prep races 18 days earlier; Combs Ditch winning a 2½ mile hurdle race around Cheltenham at 25-1 following his long absence, while Burrough Hill Lad and Wayward Lad had fought out a 3 mile chase at Wetherby. On that occasion Wayward Lad had tucked in behind Burrough Hill Lad and was well trounced by an easy 10 lengths. This time tactics would be different.

As the tapes went up and the runners went on their way, everyone in the packed stands could see that this time Wayward Lad would be taking on Burrough Hill Lad right from the beginning.

At the second, third and fourth fences this great pair rose together, providing steeplechase fans with the greatest of spectacles. At the fifth fence Wayward Lad far out jumped his illustrious rival, but they were locked together again at the next and the one after that, jumping in unison in a breathtaking display of chasing at its finest. Indeed there was barely anything between them as they passed the expectant thousands in the grandstand for the first time with Combs Ditch, the forgotten man of the party, only two lengths away and going just as easily.

Together the two great horses flew over the water jump and set out on the final circuit with the crowds thrilling at each spectacular leap. As they soared over the third of the ditches, Robert Earnshaw was seen to give Wayward Lad a smack with the whip to keep him up to his work. Was it possible that the fast pace was taking its toll and he was being run off his feet? Certainly the many supporters of Burrough Hill Lad could sense an easy victory now that the main opposition was being emphatically dealt with.

Jumping the 14th fence, only five from home, Earnshaw again had to remind the old champion four, five, six times. The old warrior responded to the urgent message as best he could, soaring over the fifteenth fence upsides his adversary to take the lead again approaching the turn into the home straight for the last time, but, unfortunately, for Wayward Lad, the writing was on the wall.

At this point Burrough Hill Lad began to quicken the pace again to go past Wayward Lad and leave his old rival toiling forlornly in his wake, a beaten horse.

Almost unnoticed until now, Combs Ditch had been drawing steadily closer to the two leaders, going past the tired Wayward Lad at the final turn. Now, with just three fences left to jump, Colin Brown switched Combs Ditch to the inside and began to deliver his challenge.

Burrough Hill Lad had only been beaten once, on his seasonal reappearance, in his last nine races, but now he would have to call on all his undoubted strength and courage to win this time from the flying Combs Ditch.

At the second last fence, John Francome was working hard on Burrough Hill Lad with only a single, fast closing, length separating the two gladiators. Hard driven, both horses answered valiantly as they bore down on the final obstacle.

They jumped the last together to a huge roar from the crowds, Burrough Hill Lad jumping just the better and getting away fractionally faster, but Combs Ditch would not be denied as they battled it out up the run in, locked together in a desperate fight for the line.

Supporters of each found themselves cheering for both gallant horses as first one, then the other had his head fractionally in front, the outcome seemingly depending on the nod at the line.

Francome asked his champion for even more effort as only he could and somehow Burrough Hill Lad found the extra strength to answer his calls yet again and get his exhausted head in front at the line to win by the shortest margin with Wayward Lad finishing, almost unnoticed, a distance back in third place.

It was, perhaps, two races within one race, with most people only remembering the brilliant, driving finish of Burrough Hill Lad and Combs Ditch, rather than the challenge valiantly thrown down by Wayward Lad over the first 2½ miles, but true lovers of steeple chasing knew that there were indeed three heroes on that glorious afternoon.

Wayward Lad, having played his part to the full was only third, but he would be back the following year to claim the prize for a record third time with Combs Ditch once again the runner up in a closely fought battle to the line.

On this day Burrough Hill Lad had claimed the spoils and standing alone in a deserted grandstand many years later, it doesn't take much imagination to still be able to hear hoarse voices screaming and see the ghosts of these equine giants fighting again. Everyone will remember the three heroes who took part for the real winners were the legions who witnessed this great race.

CRISP

At this time of year all thoughts turn to the Grand National. It still retains it's claim to be the most famous race in the world but it is by no means the supreme test that it used to be. Nowadays Becher's no longer has an open brook or that famous, dreaded drop on the landing side. In fact all of the drops have been levelled out and the fences seem to disintegrate if a horse brushes through them.

The purists would say that thirty or more years ago the fences took some real jumping and the drops would catch out the unwary. Go back even further than this and the fences were more upright still. Modification has been an element of the Aintree fences down the years for they were at one time downright dangerous.

Go back to November 1919 and both the Beecher Chase and the Valentine Chase were declared void for no horse finished either race. This was the fifth time the big Aintree fences had failed to produce a single finisher.

Was the five times Cheltenham Gold Cup winner, Golden Miller, the greatest National horse when he broke the course record? Perhaps Bullingdon, trained by George Owen, who, in 1948, fell at the first but got up and jumped the rest of the course unaided and finished ahead of the first ridden runner. Davy Jones was set to win when his reins broke at the very last fence and he ran out, Russian Hero nearly died of colic before his heroic victory and Devon Loch, in 1956, was set to break the course record when he collapsed with cramp on the run in. Of the more recent generations perhaps West Tip should be included but we'll look at the 1973 running for the answer to the poser of who is the greatest National horse of them all.

There seemed to be three main principles among the 38 runners for the race run on 31st March 1973. Dual Cheltenham Gold Cup winner,

L'Escargot was a best priced 11/1 under his burden of 12 stone.

Joint top weight was the 9/1 joint favourite, Crisp, a massive, nearly black, gelding standing 17.1hh. The other joint favourite, carrying just 10 stone 5 pounds was Ginger McCain's runner, Red Rum.

Some of the other notables included former winner, Black Secret, Whitbread winner, Grey Sombrero, and prolific winner, Spanish Steps, while the most intriguing competitor was the 54 year old Duke of Alburqueque riding his own horse, Nereo.

By far the most interesting horse in the field was Fred Winter's Crisp. In his native Australia he won races on the Flat over 10 furlongs and 1m5f. Switched to fences he won the Melbourne Chase and the Carolina Hunt Cup in Camden USA.

His owner/breeder, Sir Chester Manifold, brought him to England where he began his career with a 15 length romp at Wincanton and just 5 days later won the 2 mile Champion Chase at Cheltenham by 25 lengths. The season after that he won several races at 3 miles, including what is now the Racing Post Chase, giving weight and a beating to possibly the strongest field in the races history and then finished 4th in the Gold Cup, clearly not staying the distance.

The following season he campaigned with the 2 mile crown again in mind and started a hard odds on favourite when finishing 3rd to Inkslinger. And so this brilliant 2 miler, who had class to win over 3 miles was set to tackle the 30 huge fences spread over 4½ miles of Aintree.

As the tapes rose and the field set off towards the first fence it was Grey Sombrero on the outside, Black Secret in the centre and Crisp on the nearside. All three easily clearing the first five fences, line across the course.

Richard Pitman, Crisp's jockey intended to make the running and slow the pace from the front but soon found that Crisp was accelerating as he approached each fence, really attacking them, then being steadied by Pitman until he caught sight of the next obstacle and he was off again.

Going into Beecher's Brook for the first time Grey Sombrero held a slight lead but Crisp met it on a perfect stride and landed so far out the other side he cleared the fearsome drop and landed on level ground. By the next Crisp now had four lengths to spare over Grey Sombrero and this is how they stayed over the Canal Turn and Valentine's Brook, Endless Folly and Black Secret next with Red Rum in about 10th place.

As they raced back towards the grandstand Crisp had extended his lead to eight lengths with a further 6 lengths between Grey Sombrero and the rest of the field.

At the Chair Crisp was a full 15 lengths clear from Grey Sombrero who had a bad fall and tragically broke a shoulder.

Tommy Stack, who would later partner Red Rum to Grand National glory, was injured and watching the race from the stands commented: "Jesus. There's no way he can keep up that pace for so long".

Indeed, at the finishing post on the first circuit Crisp would normally be finishing his races but he had another circuit to go at the 2 mile pace he was inflicting on his pursuers.

Racing out onto the second circuit with 25 of the 38 runners still standing, Crisp was now 25 lengths clear of Rouge Autumn with Red Rum now deciding to give chase to the disappearing shape in the distance.

Commentator Julian Wilson intoned: "I can't remember a horse so far ahead in the Grand National at this stage".

On and on Crisp ran, jumping like a stag, a joy to watch, while Red Rum toiled away the best part of a fence behind with Spanish Steps 6 lengths behind him. Fence after fence Crisp soared perfectly under his massive weight, giving over two and a half stone to his pursuer, who was slowly starting to close the gap on the runaway leader.

Over three out and 15 lengths still separate Crisp from Red Rum but Pitman takes a quick look round. Red Rum is under pressure but this one signal that perhaps Crisp's tank was emptying galvanised Brian Fletcher to keep asking Red Rum for more.

With two to jump trainer Fred Winter, who had watched the race in total silence so far, turned to Crisp's owner, Sir Chester Manifold, and said: "Start praying now, Sir Chester, for you're going to be beat".

Pitman knew he was riding what was basically a non-stayer and had to keep hold of his head for as long as he could, for the moment a non-stayer comes off the bridle and you start pushing, you are in trouble.

When you have an out-and-out stayer, like Red Rum, you can push for ever and they will keep finding more.

At the penultimate fence Crisp gave a split second stagger as exhaustion started to take hold. The gap was still dwindling but Crisp still led by 12 lengths. The last fence and Crisp was getting very tired but still had the race at his mercy with just the 494 yard run in to go.

As they approached the elbow Pitman made a basic error and used his whip right handed, sending Crisp left away from the whip and off a true line. Pitman maintains that this is what made the difference between winning and losing, not the weight he carried.

With only a furlong left to run Crisp had slowed almost to a walk as Red Rum surged towards him. Crisp heard Red Rum coming and tried to go again but he was just too tired. In the shadow of the post Red Rum reached Crisp to win by a mere ¾ of a length. Radio commentator Peter Bromley expounding: "Red Rum snatches the National, Crisp is second and the rest don't matter for we will never see another race like that in a hundred years".

Richard Pitman first felt desolation but that was quickly followed by elation as no-one had ever had a ride round Aintree like that.

The course record, set by Golden Miller in 1934 had been shattered by nearly 19 seconds. A monumental feat. For the record L'Escargot was 25 lengths behind in 3rd place with a further 12 lengths back to Spanish Steps in 4th.

Crisp soon recovered and easily thrashed Red Rum the next time they met but on this day he only just failed to give the most successful Aintree jumper in history 23 pounds. At level weights there can be no doubt as to who the greatest Grand National horse has to be.

Red Rum got his name on the roll of honour for the first of an unprecedented three times but the 1973 race will forever be remembered as "Crisp's National".

TINGLE CREEK

The beauty of horseracing in this country is the incredible difference in tracks and settings available, especially in the National Hunt sphere. Unlike certain countries where all the racecourses are identical, here the geography caters for every possible whim or taste.

Although unliked by many jockeys, few courses can match the surrounding scenery of Plumpton on a sunny day, or perhaps the natural amphitheatre of Cheltenham, while a trip to the course by boat can be arranged at some courses.

On an equine front the idiosyncrasies of horses are catered for by left hand courses, right hand courses and even a figure of eight at Fontwell. Tight, flat tracks like Kempton suit some horses while the wide galloping course at Newbury may suit others. Equally the undulations of Exeter favour some horses, the never ending 4 furlong run from the last fence at Cartmel favours others, the stiff fences at Haydock are best attempted by precise jumpers while Chepstow is best suited to its own particular type of course specialists.

In short, there is a racecourse somewhere in this country to suit every type of horse or spectator.

In 1972 an exciting American prospect who had won several major steeplechases in the USA was sent to Newmarket trainer Harry Thomson Jones. This chestnut gelding was a particularly fast and fluent jumper for which Sandown Park, and particularly the railway fences down the far side, seemed tailor made for the horse. As the closest line of fences anywhere in the country they could prove very tricky for a slow or inexperienced jumper but a fast, confident, attacking beast could often gain a decisive advantage before the turn into the home straight.

This horse was Tingle Creek and the Sandown Pattern Chase over 2 miles would prove to be, without doubt, his speciality event.

Tingle Creek's sire, Goose Creek, had run in England, proving fast enough to win the Champagne Stakes at Salisbury and finish second in the Royal Lodge at Ascot. Tingle Creek's dam, Martingale, won three races on the flat in America while her sire, Flushing II, had success in France, winning the Prix Carlos on the flat in 1942 before a jumping career took his win tally to 17 from 63 starts before his later career at stud.

Foaled in America in 1966 Tingle Creek's major successes in America had both been over 2½ miles, breaking the Belmont course record in the process and then finishing a good third to the top American chaser of the time over 3 miles, but his future lay in the far more competitive world of racing in England and Ireland.

Tingle Creek acquitted himself well enough in his first races here before being sent to Sandown Park for the first time in November 1973 where he was electrifying, leaving his rivals for dead as he thrashed Spanish Steps and the others by 10 lengths and more in a new course record time.

Further victories followed at Sandown, Nottingham and Doncaster before Tingle Creek was sent off an odds-on favourite in the 2 mile Champion Chase at the Cheltenham Festival. Setting off like a bullet the rest of the field were soon in trouble until Tingle Creek clouted the eighth fence so hard he lost all momentum. To his eternal credit he rallied gamely to take second place in this Championship race on a course he clearly loathed for the rest of his career.

At Punchestown 6 weeks later he gave subsequent dual 2 mile Champion Chase winner Skymas 16lbs and a 6 length thrashing.

The following season Tingle Creek ran three brilliant races in defeat at Sandown, coming second in a close finish to Pendil when receiving only one pound, then finding the brilliant Dorlesa just too good when giving the winner 30lbs and finally just succumbing to Bula at level weights.

By now the Sandown crowds had adopted Tingle Creek as their own warrior and every time he ran there he had a huge following. In all, Tingle Creek was to run at Sandown 12 times, including six appearances in the Sandown Pattern Chase. Recording five victories, five second places, a third and a fourth place from those dozen course appearances,

Tingle Creek set a second course record when winning the Pattern Chase again in 1977 where he led from start to finish under Steve Smith-Eccles and held Perambulate up the final hill when giving the runner up 21lbs.

Smith-Eccles recounts; "He broke fast from the gate and if horses could have a recognisable grin on their faces I swear his would have stretched from ear to ear as he was unleashed towards the first obstacle. The jumping was what he loved. He was fast, brave and as extravagant a leaper as any horse I have ever sat on".

Smith-Eccles later added; "He either met a fence long or even longer! He would never get in close and fiddle. He never fell in 49 starts and certainly with me I can't even remember him making a mistake".

As a 12 year old Tingle Creek recorded two wins and a second from the opening three races of his final campaign.

Tom Jones had pre-planned his last race and retirement for November 4th 1978 when he would contest the Sandown Pattern Chase for the last time. With two wins and three second places in the previous five runnings of the race it was an apt choice.

With thousands more on the gate to see their hero make his farewell performance, Tingle Creek was sent off at 7/2, the second choice in the betting market.

It was no surprise that Tingle Creek led from the start at a million miles per hour where to see him jumping the railway fences was a privilege and an honour. With the small field strung out behind and just three fences left to jump Tingle Creek soared over the Pond fence and the crowd rose as one to cheer him on. He met the last in his stride and powered up the hill for the final time with every voice raised in salute to win again. Just to put the icing on the cake, old Tingle Creek broke his own course record yet again!

Sporting Life race reporter, Len Thomas, wrote; "Not since the days of Arkle have I witnessed an ovation such as that accorded Tingle Creek at Sandown on Saturday…it was a real fairy tale ending. The crowd, sensing victory as Tingle Creek fairly flew the Pond fence, the third from home, urged him on. Their roars reached a crescendo as the old horse, still full of running, fairly pinged the last, leaving the others in his wake. On that last day at Sandown they cheered him every step of the path back to the familiar winners' enclosure, to an emotional owner and a misty-eyed trainer".

Tingle Creek had won his 23rd and final victory, in eighteen of which he carried 12 stone or more, with successes gained at no less than ten different courses and was placed on his only appearance at three other tracks.

!n 1979 the Sandown Park executive renamed the Pattern Chase in his honour and that name, "The Tingle Creek Chase", still stands proudly today as a fitting reminder of a great horse.

For many years Tingle Creek paraded in front of the stands before each running of the race named after him and more often than not spectators in the stands ignored the days' runners as they pointed out Tingle Creek and said; "You know who that is? That's Tingle Creek! What a horse he was round here".

His last appearance at Sandown was in 1995 where he still drew warm applause from the crowds and nodding affection from those who remembered his glory days.

Tingle Creek died the following year at the age of 30.

Remembered not only by the race named in his honour but wherever people meet and talk of the greatest horse ever seen tackling Sandown's railway fences, the legend that was Tingle Creek.

PERSIAN WAR

At the very start of the golden age of hurdling Persian War was the first in a long line of superstars. Running a bit before I was old enough to take a keen interest in the sport all I really knew subsequently was that Persian War was good and his owner was regarded as bad. Was this a myth or reality?

Foaled on March 24 1963 at the Cloghan Stud in Dublin the small bay colt received special injections to help a weakness in his legs which would plague his later life.

Originally trained on the flat by Dick Hern, Persian War managed to win a couple of moderate long distance races before it was decided his future lay over timber. Offered to several National Hunt trainers and rejected each time he eventually ended up at Newmarket Tattersalls sales where Lewes trainer Tom Masson paid 3600 guineas for the gelding.

A second place and two wins from his first three races left Masson so certain he had a star on his hands that he heavily backed the three year old to win the Champion Hurdle four months later!

Persian War's owner, the oil tanker magnate, Donald Leyland-Naylor no longer went racing due to serious illness and decided to sell his horses. A month later middle aged businessman Henry Alper saw Persian War run in a televised race at Newbury and was immediately impressed with the way his long stride devoured his opponents in the straight and although far from fluent over his obstacles he still won unchallenged by 8 lengths.

Former jockey, Brian Swift, had recently set up as a trainer and Alper had been introduced to him by Swift's bookmaker father, Jack. Having always been interested in racing, Alper made the sudden decision to purchase this, his first horse and instructed Swift to buy him.

Canny businessman Tom Masson, representing the owner, famously responded to this enquiry about Persian War by stating; "You can buy anything from me except my mother." And so, for the record price for a hurdler at that time of £9,000 Alper had the horse he had set his sights on.

The Challow hurdle at Newbury on January 13 1966 was Alper's first race as an owner and it was a winning one as Persian War came with a late run under Jimmy Uttley to win with a ton in hand. A facile victory at Kempton was followed by a trip to Haydock for the Victor Ludorum, one of the most valuable events in the calendar. Three of the first five flights of hurdles were flattened yet between the last two even the racecourse commentator intoned; "Persian War is cantering in front and nothing can possibly catch him" as he recorded yet another contemptuously easy victory. Alper, with three wins from his first three races as an owner, was spot on in his description of Persian War's hurdling ability when he later said; "If the obstacles were in the right place for him when he jumped he cleared them with fluency and precision, if not he would either go through them or knock them over without a break in his pace-devouring stride."

In this first season hurdling Persian War set the tone for what was to come. An incredibly gentle and well behaved horse at home, Swift's five year old daughter was often led round the yard perched on his back, Persian War would do anything asked of him on the gallops, but generally in his own time, and ate, well, like a horse, consuming twenty pounds of corn every day. In his races Persian War took a while to warm up, treated the obstacles with disdain and then stormed through to win his races with a rare courage and determination.

Alper was like a kid with a much loved new toy. His adoration of Persian War was astounding, visiting what was really a pet to him at every opportunity and, unfortunately, telephoning his trainer two or three times every day to ask about his welfare and formulate future plans.

Alper, not to mention Tom Masson, was very keen to run in the Champion Hurdle but Brian Swift persuaded Alper to keep to the novice route this season. The racing press then rounded on Swift to aim for the big one, citing the fact that all his wins were in very fast times. Swift's classic response was; "We take no notice of times in this country; we leave that to the Americans!"

Prior to Cheltenham Persian War ran at Kempton, a course totally unsuitable to his long striding, galloping action. Just behind the leaders at the last in the back straight Persian War pitched forward on landing and smacked his head hard on the ground, losing all impetus but still running on to take third place. In the unsaddling enclosure blood was pouring from a gaping wound in his tongue and two teeth were now missing.

The Triumph hurdle was the first time Persian War had raced on a firm surface and many doubted his ability to produce the form he had shown on soft and heavy going. As it transpired Persian War seemed even better; his hurdling was superb for a change and he pulled strongly up the hill to win well in a manner which would certainly have won the Champion Hurdle itself if he had contested that race instead.

A long summer's rest at Harry Carr's Genesis Green Stud saw Persian War grow and mature and generally thrive on the rich pasture.

Following a warm up on the flat he stripped fitter for his first race of the new term at Newbury against a highly regarded hotpot in Mugatpurn. Unbeaten in all four races and receiving 7lbs counted for nothing as Persian War was let loose before the seventh flight and quickly put daylight between the two, cantering to an easy 25 length win.

Next up was Cheltenham where heavy rain had produced such atrocious going it was surprising it hadn't been abandoned as unraceable. Going as well as any in the mire Persian War took an horrendous fall two out, sliding yards along the muddy turf. Running from the stands, Alper and Swift found Jimmy Uttley cradling the still head of Persian War in his lap, tears running down his face, convinced the worst had happened. Luckily Persian War had only knocked himself out and some minutes later struggled back to his feet, surprised but at least in one piece.

Shortly after this an epidemic of foot and mouth closed racing down. Alper and Swift were considering sending Persian War to race in France when Alper found out the French would be banning British horses entering the country a few days later. Quickly he arranged for a horse box to collect his horse for shipping to a French trainer but couldn't get through to Swift to advise him. When the box turned up the following morning Swift turned it away and ordered Alper to remove his horses. Alper tried to repair the damage but Swift was adamant. Recounting his memories many years later Alper was adamant that for Persian War's early years he couldn't have been in better hands than with Swift.

Alper decided to send his horses to the Chepstow trainer Colin Davies. Two excellent efforts in defeat saw Persian War line up next for the Schweppes at Newbury, the richest handicap hurdle in Europe. Carrying 11.13 in a field of 33 Persian War put up arguably his best performance, up with the pace, leading on the run in, headed close home then battling back to claim victory on the line in a thrilling contest.

The Champion Hurdle of 1968 turned into an Alper procession. The horse he had leased from his trainers' father set the required strong gallop until Persian War took it up approaching two out, easily fighting off the only two horses able to get close enough to mount a challenge.

At the end of the season Persian War was overwhelmingly voted National Hunt Horse of the Year, the first hurdler ever to be so honoured.

Two excellent efforts in France preceded a race at Worcester which almost ended his career. Looking every inch the winner he slipped on landing after the fifth and suffered a small fracture of the femur which sidelined him for some months.

February 1969 saw his comeback race at Kempton. Clearly far from fit, giving the best part of two stone to the other runners and with connections worried how the leg would stand up at racing pace, Persian War started at 10/1. Incredibly he jumped brilliantly, pulled himself into the lead and stayed there to win by 3 lengths to rapturous applause. An American owner who witnessed the race immediately offered Alper $250,000 for his horse and was turned down without a second thought.

The Schweppes was lost to the weather so Davies chose the Kingwell hurdle at Wincanton as the next target. A pricked hoof combined with an allergic reaction to penicillin left Persian War with a temperature of 103 degrees the day before the race. Henry Alper was concerned not only for his horse but also for the many thousands making the pilgrimage to see him run. The vet gave a thumbs up the following morning and Davies was happy enough although Uttley knew his mount wasn't right as he walked round the paddock. In light of this, second place was an admirable performance.

The Cheltenham Festival was lucky to survive the heavy rains which had already wiped out racing across the country for several days. As usual the Irish had a "banker" at the meeting, in this case the mud loving L'Escargot who would also be contesting the Champion Hurdle. It didn't really matter though as Persian War was imperious in landing his second successive title.

Three weeks later the ground was rock hard for the Welsh equivalent at Chepstow. Again it mattered not as Persian War was never off a tight rein to win as he pleased and to cap a wonderful season he was again voted National Hunt Horse of the Year.

After another couple of races in France Persian War had another race on the flat in a handicap at Newbury in September which resulted in an over-reach and splint trouble which would keep him off the racetrack for another three months. Davies was out of the country when Alper declared the horse to run and blamed the injury on Alper's need for a lightweight jockey to do the required 7.2 not being able to hold him properly. Perhaps this is a sleight on a horse with no vices and a young Pat Eddery!

A further comeback race at Sandown then threw up yet another problem, this time with his wind. Davies had been aware of a growing difficulty for a while but this time Persian War was gurgling badly and swallowing his tongue to such an extent that Uttley nearly pulled him up before his wind cleared and he ran on well into second place.

A tongue strap was used for the first time in a brand new race at Fairyhouse, the Irish Sweeps Hurdle. Half a mile out Persian War gurgled again and quickly lost his place before recovering his breath and improving to third place at the last flight. Uttley sent his mount for a gap between the leaders which was abruptly closed as he went for it leaving him nowhere to go. After finishing an unlucky third it was incredible that no Stewards Enquiry was called.

Haydock Park in January 1970 was the venue for the first time, barring falls, that Persian War had ever finished out of the first three. Davies had inexplicably decided to see if the tongue strap made that much difference and left it off only for the horse to swallow his tongue at halfway and trail home in 12th place.

This was followed by two fantastic races in defeat where Uttley rode the finishes with just hands and heels as instructed, yet the press cited his successive defeats since the previous March as proof he was a spent force. The press also spread the rumour that Uttley would be replaced by Bob Davies for the Champion Hurdle at which Alper immediately phoned his distraught jockey to tell him it was complete nonsense.

At Cheltenham Persian War and Uttley were back to their very best. Taking the lead a mile from home Persian War did it the hard way. Seriously challenged time and again by six different horses he repelled everything thrown at him to secure a fourth consecutive Festival victory and a third Champion Hurdle.

Alper watched the final furlong from the stands with tears running unheeded down his cheeks, the victor then receiving three heartfelt cheers in the winners enclosure. Persian War's three Champion Hurdles had now been won on firm, good and heavy going and a third National Hunt Horse of the Year title was just a formality.

Over the years Alper had received dozens of cards and letters from well wishers. This grew to hundreds as Persian War entered Newmarket's Equine Research Centre for operations on his soft palate, wolf teeth, a hook tooth and two fractured molars. Despite enormous blood loss the operations were successful and he quickly recovered.

In the June of 1970 Davies instructed Alper to remove all his horses after Alper had tried to sell another horse against his trainers wishes. Alper requested that Davies keep Persian War due to their successful association but Davies stipulated certain rules and conditions which Alper found unacceptable. In following press releases Alper went out of his way to express his "sincere thanks to Colin Davies, the lads and everyone previously connected with Persian War".

Next Persian War was sent to Dennis Rayston as he trained close to the Equine Centre in Newmarket and returned to him after a period with Arthur Pitt, a young trainer with only a few horses who Alper had kindly promised would be sent Persian War to make his dream come true if he ever left Colin Davies.

The 1970/71 season saw Persian War make his latest comeback at Ludlow a winning one. Other top performances included winning the Irish Sweeps Hurdle before a first meeting with the unbeaten rising star, Bula. Second by 10 lengths but giving the younger horse 4lbs set the scene for the Champion Hurdle a month later.

At Cheltenham Persian War jumped past his pacemaker at the second last and fought off the challengers around him but Bula was stalking the field on the outside. The old king battling on bravely to hold second place but Bula had flown the last to retain his unbeaten record, win the crown and usher in a new era.

Persian War's leg problems persisted over the following seasons and finally ended his career as an eleven year old before a tilt at the County Hurdle.

So, was Persian War a good horse and Henry Alper a bad owner?

In my opinion Alper was a man who clearly loved his horse but, new to racehorse ownership, was terribly naïve and in wanting to be involved caused a few frictions which he unfairly bore the sole blame for.

For relentless, grinding power on any going, a fantastic attitude and will to win even when beset with so many ailments and injuries together with a record that speaks for itself, Persian War must rate as one of the greatest hurdlers the sport has been honoured to know.

Retired to a well deserved life of leisure back at Harry Carr's stud, Persian War had a contented retirement until his legs became so bad he could barely move. In September 1984, at the age of 21, Persian War was quietly put to sleep.

His heart is buried under a headstone Alper had erected at the stud.

VIKING FLAGSHIP

It happens every now and then that two great horses conspire to present us with a race to remember for many years. How rare it is that three champions should be at the top of their game in the same race and perform to the best of their form.

The contrast in these goliaths of the equine world for this clash of the titans was exceptional. The super tough, uncompromising bruiser who liked nothing more than to slug it out toe to toe with his rivals and pound them into submission; the fragile but unbeaten speed merchant whose turn of foot had always proved decisive; finally the tenacious terrier who would come again and again until victory was assured.

To that end we look at the 2½ mile Melling Chase run at level weights at Aintree on 7 April 1995.

For the fragile but unbeaten speed merchant we have arguably Tim Forster's best ever horse, Martha's Son.

Going into the race Martha's Son had won all nine of his chase starts to date. Starting modestly as a novice the previous season Martha's Son had three straight victories under his belt before being upped in class for his last race of the season at Sandown. In the present campaign he was aimed much higher and would start to come up against the best around, including of course Viking Flagship and Deep Sensation.

An easy victory first time out at Haydock was followed by a trip to Huntingdon for their prestigious 2½ mile Peterborough Chase where Martha's Son beat Deep Sensation by just over a length when in receipt of 9lbs. Another facile victory at Wincanton was then followed by a crack at the big guns over 2 miles in the Victor Chandler Chase at Ascot. On only 10.9 Martha's Son cruised to an easy victory with the heavily laden Viking Flagship and Deep Sensation finishing together 27 lengths adrift of the winner. Another crack at 2½ miles in Ascot's Comet Chase saw 7 lengths between Martha's Son and his nearest pursuer with Deep Sensation 20 lengths back in fourth place. Bypassing Cheltenham this year the unbeaten new talent would start 11/10 favourite at Aintree. Although injury would interrupt his later career, Martha's Son would later win Cheltenham's 2 mile Champion Chase and Aintree's Melling Chase in the future, beating a battle weary Viking Flagship on both occasions.

As the tenacious terrier and proven expert at the distance, take Josh Gifford's Deep Sensation.

Only two years earlier Deep Sensation had been crowned Champion Chaser over 2 miles at the Cheltenham Festival and followed that up with victory in this same Melling Chase at Aintree.

At 10 years old Deep Sensation was conceding 2 years to both his principal opponents yet was far from a back number. After a pipe opener at Exeter Deep Sensation won at Cheltenham before the Peterborough Chase against Martha's Son. He then finished 5 lengths third to Viking Flagship in the Tingle Creek at Sandown before meeting the same horse in the Castleford Chase at Wetherby where he fell at only the fourth fence.

With the exception of a fifth place in a King George at Kempton, Deep Sensation had never finished lower than fourth in all his completed chase starts, so it seems fair to say this fall may have affected his confidence a little as he finished only 6th next time out in the Victor Chandler at Ascot well behind Martha's Son and finishing only a neck adrift of Viking Flagship who was carrying 7lbs more.

Next up was the Comet Chase before another crack at the 2 mile Champion Chase where only Viking Flagship finished ahead of him albeit by 7 lengths.

The Melling Chase would prove to be his last race, for which he would start at 5/1.

For super tough bruiser it could only ever be Viking Flagship.
With the great Northern Dancer as his paternal grandsire great things were expected of Viking Flagship who ran without winning 4 times as a two-year-old and 14 more times at three at distances from 7f to 1m6f.

Tony Holdsworth, his owner, then sent him to Martin Pipe where he

soon got the hang of things and won the last four of his 6 starts before Holdsworth decided to sell him to Graham Roach.
The first Pipe knew of this was when the vet turned up for the pre-sale check and found him lame, although he did pass two days later and was promptly moved to David Nicholson's yard.

Nicholson understood his new inmate very well and quickly realised what a stuffy horse he was and the incredible amount of work required to get him right and a horse of a lesser constitution would never have thrived in the way Viking Flagship did.

After a decent novice chase season in which he even won twice in 3 days at the Punchestown Festival meeting, Viking Flagship really started to make an impact the following season. Only third of four in the betting for the Victor Chandler Chase behind his more illustrious stable companion, Waterloo Boy and Egypt Mill Prince it was these two who had drawn clear with only three left to jump with Viking Flagship looking beaten. Perhaps for the first time we saw what he was really made of as he rallied and battled in a manner which would prove to be his trademark to take the race close home. Next up for Viking Flagship was the Game Spirit Chase at Newbury where the reigning two mile champion chaser, Deep Sensation and the brilliant Sybillin were both going far better in the closing stages but again the doughty Flagship out battled his rivals to take the spoils.

At Cheltenham in 1994 for the Champion Chase a line of three jumped the last together, Viking Flagship on the inside, Deep Sensation in the middle and the previous season's Arkle winner, Travado, going easily best of all on the outside. In easily the race of the meeting Viking Flagship again prevailed by a neck.

The following season he was reportedly not right when he was trounced by Martha's Son in the Victor Chandler before retaining his 2 mile crown at the main expense of Deep Sensation. Going into the Aintree race over a distance he had never won at before, Viking Flagship started at 5/2.

Although there were three other runners in the race, all eyes would be on the three principles, the reigning champion, Viking Flagship, the unbeaten pretender to the throne, Martha's Son and a former champion,

Deep Sensation, who had been deemed a certainty for this race by Josh Gifford, his trainer.

On a lovely sunny day Nakir set off in front for the first three fences, Martha's Son making a slight mistake at the second, then Southolt took up the running while Second Schedule jumped poorly and struggled from the outset.

Southolt bravely led on the rails with Viking Flagship tracking him, Martha's Son seemingly glued to his principle rival and watching his every move, Nakir tucked in behind the leading trio while Deep Sensation stalked them all. Second Schedule was already 10 lengths adrift and would soon be pulled up.

With four fences left to jump in this intriguing contest Southolt still held a small advantage over Viking Flagship with a bare length to the other three, racing line abreast. Round the home turn and three out the race was beginning in earnest, Southold still leading but coming under strong pressure, Viking Flagship bearing down while Martha's Son was none too fluent on the stands side. Nakir was being hard driven to close on the leader while Deep Sensation still tracked these but was also closing.

On the run to the penultimate fence Nakir cracked under the pressure and dropped away, the other four all under strong driving jumped it well, Southolt touching down marginally in front as Viking Flagship and Martha's Son both powered up alongside, Deep Sensation only inches away on the far side. Between the last two Southolt can find no more...he's run a brave race but cedes the lead to Viking Flagship only for Martha's Son to edge past into the lead a few strides later. Bearing down on the last fence the commentator summed it up exactly; "This is everything you've ever dreamt of".

At the last and the big three jump it together, Martha's Son touching down fractionally in front from Deep Sensation storming up on the far side, Viking Flagship between the two. Deep Sensation continues his surging run and starts to pull ahead, Martha's Son can't seem to find any more and Viking Flagship also looks beat. Deep Sensation pulls half a length to the good on the short run to the winning post while Martha's Son starts to rally and close on the leader, Viking Flagship fractionally in third place now also starts to fight like only he can and together they claw back Deep Sensation, but Deep Sensation isn't stopping. Martha's Son can go no faster and is beaten but Viking Flagship rallies again, this super tough animal who doesn't know the meaning of defeat. In one last surge Viking Flagship and Deep Sensation cross the line together, Martha's Son a bare length away in third place. Having never lost a photo finish Viking Flagship wasn't going to start now and his equally tough jockey, Adrian Maguire, punched the air in triumph as Viking Flagship prevailed by the narrowest of margins in easily the best race of the season.

Both Maguire and Richard Dunwoody hailed Viking Flagship as the toughest horse they had ever ridden, while trainer David Nicholson summed it up; "He's the toughest horse I've ever trained. The amount of work that he stands would kill most people".

Having won the Melling Chase the following year as well, Viking Flagship was honourably retired in 1998. It was expected that after so many tough battles Viking Flagship would live a long and happy retirement in the paddocks but tragedy struck only two years later when he broke a leg in those same paddocks and had to be put down.

Although a true champion in his own right it was his battling qualities that set him apart. First the Champion Chase at Cheltenham in 1994 and then, in 1995, that incredible battle of the champions for the Melling Chase at Aintree sealed his epitaph for all time...simply the toughest horse there ever was.

BROWNE'S GAZETTE

If you compiled a shortlist of the best hurdlers never to have won the Champion Hurdle Birds Nest would be top of most lists, but who else would be on it?

Celtic Ryde, Ekbalco, the ill fated Golden Cygnet? In more recent years Large Action and even Harchibald would figure on a lot of lists yet one name would be continually overlooked, despite his undoubted brilliance, through no fault of his own.

Horseracing in this country is almost entirely straight and far removed from the corrupt picture painted in some racing novels or prevalent in some other countries. It is with horror, then, that we react when a well known jockey riding for a top stable is found to be irrefutably guilty of doping horses and other evil doing to such an extent that he is prosecuted by the police and warned off for life by the racing authorities.

For that jockey to be linked inextricably with a particular horse is why that animal is tarnished to the point of being totally forgotten by the racing world. That horse was Browne's Gazette and the evil doing jockey was his former owner, Dermot Browne.

To pay Browne's Gazette his due and to see what the Dickinson trained gelding was capable of we look today at Kempton Park's prestigious Christmas Hurdle of 1984.

Browne's Gazette, running now in the ownership of John Poynton, was in his second season of racing and was already hyped up as potentially one of the best hurdlers ever seen.

As a juvenile Browne's Gazette won his first ever race by an easy 12 lengths at odds of 10/11 against 16 opponents at Wetherby. Then at 1/7 and 1/5 he won his next two with consummate ease by 20 lengths on both occasions before tipping up at the last when well in control on his next outing. Normal service was resumed with another 20 length procession before he lined up at Cheltenham for the Supreme Novices Hurdle, the only race of the season where he would not start odds on. It made no difference as he sauntered up the Cheltenham hill by a very comfortable 10 lengths before finishing his season with another easy victory at the big Aintree meeting.

In the current campaign a far from race fit Browne's Gazette went down by 2 lengths to the smart Ballydurrow, who was receiving 8lbs, in Newcastle's Ekbalco hurdle but gained revenge three weeks later on the same course in the Fighting Fifth where Ballydurrow received 9lbs and a 6 length thrashing with a distance back to the third horse.

Next up for Browne's Gazette was a trip back to Cheltenham for the Bula hurdle against the former Champion hurdler, Gaye Brief, who had been backed into 4/11 against the new kid on the block. Receiving 6lbs on this occasion, Browne's Gazette made the former champion look one paced as he cruised up the hill with Gaye Brief toiling 8 lengths behind in second place.

On December 26th 1984 Browne's Gazette would face possibly his biggest test to date.

Second favourite in the field of seven at 2/1 was John Francome's mount, See You Then. The previous season See You Then had won three of his four races, his only defeat was in coming second in the Triumph hurdle at the Cheltenham Festival.

In this campaign See You Then had opened with a commendable third behind Ra Nova in the Gerry Fielden hurdle at Newbury before a trip to Ascot where he gave a stone and a 2 length beating to the previously unbeaten Joy Ride, with a patently unfit Desert Orchid 5 lengths further away.

An interesting point in the career of See You Then is that in all he achieved over the years his Italian owner, the Marquis Cugliemi di Vulci, who ran him under the name of his Stype Wood Stud, never once saw him race...a detriment to a great horse.

Well supported at 3/1 for the Christmas Hurdle was the front running Ra Nova who preceded his defeat of See You Then at Newbury with another victory at Kempton over Janus, Desert Orchid and the smart

Very Promising. A year before he had won the Schweppes at Newbury and the Welsh Champion hurdle at Chepstow among others.

The aforementioned Desert Orchid was next in the betting at 10/1. His two races so far this season were the level weights third place to See You Then and a similar position behind Ra Nova and Janus. No slouch over hurdles he had won the Kingwell at Wincanton and the Tolworth at Sandown the previous year among many victories for the popular front running grey.

At 25/1, Rushmoor had won his last three races before being disqualified from second spot in a hot handicap at Sandown. The mare Stan's Pride had been behind Browne's Gazette and Gaye Brief at Cheltenham and 33/1 was a true reflection of her chances in this company while the other 33/1 shot, Janus, having split Ra Nova and Desert Orchid on his first start of the season had then won a small race at Huntingdon and run a creditable second at Ascot. On all known form the 11/8 favourite looked to just have the measure of See You Then, Ra Nova and Desert Orchid with the other three very capable but not really up to this class.

With three confirmed front runners in the field it was always going to be a fast pace and that is how it transpired as Desert Orchid shot into a three length lead over the first of the eight hurdles. Ra Nova, Rushmoor and Janus followed the leader with another three lengths back to the others.

Over the second flight, past the packed stands and onto the next they raced with Desert Orchid leading by a length now from Rushmoor and Ra Nova, Browne's Gazette had cruised up to fourth with See You Then jumping a little stickily towards the rear.

On into the back straight where Desert Orchid extended his lead to 6 lengths from a line of three; Janus, Rushmoor and Ra Nova, who could never get to the front. Two lengths behind this triumvirate came Browne's Gazette with a further length back to See You Then. The race was starting to hot up as they started the long turn into the home straight with Dermot Browne having a long look round at See You Then.

Approaching two out and Desert Orchid still led on the inside as the menacing figure of Browne's Gazette cruised up effortlessly on his outside, See You Then ridden up to third and the rest beating a retreat. After clearing the penultimate flight Dermot Browne loosed the reins on Browne's Gazette and he flew into a clear lead, swamping Desert Orchid for foot and still riding just hands and heels after the last while Colin Brown on Desert Orchid and Francome on See You Then were hard at work.

Eased up 50 yards before the line Browne's Gazette still had 15 lengths of daylight back to Desert Orchid and another 10 back to See You Then in a truly masterful performance in a very fast run race.

How good was the race though? In their next runs Desert Orchid easily won the Oteley hurdle at Sandown by 10 lengths while Ra Nova and Janus finished first and second in the listed New Years' Day hurdle at Windsor. Stan's Pride also won a modest event while later on Rushmoor was a close up 5th in the County hurdle at the Cheltenham Festival when giving lumps of weight to the rest of the field before winning next time out.

Of the principals, See You Then tuned up for Cheltenham with a cosy victory while Browne's Gazette strung out a modest field by 20, 30 and 15 lengths when giving weight away all round.

With the glory of the Champion Hurdle beckoning for the 4/6 favourite, Browne's Gazette infamously whipped round at the start of the race to lose at least 20 lengths. In a race that was to set a new course record he couldn't quite peg back this deficit and finished 6th of the 14 runners only 14 lengths adrift of See You Then, with old adversaries Stan's Pride 3rd and Gaye Brief 4th. On equal footing there could only have been one winner.

To ensure his season didn't end on a sour note Browne's Gazette went to Chepstow to contest the Welsh Champion hurdle where he recorded another easy victory despite giving weight away to all his rivals.

It was widely expected that this brilliant hurdler would sweep all before him over the coming years as he started odds on for his first outing of the new season in the Fighting Fifth. Well up with the pace early on, Browne's Gazette suddenly veered sharply right, crashing through the running rails as he died instantly from a heart attack.

It is history now that See You Then won a record equalling three

Champion hurdles at Cheltenham, yet how easily he was brushed aside at Kempton shows only what might have been. But for the tragedy that befell him, Browne's Gazette could have become the greatest hurdler of all time yet due to the unsavoury antics of his jockey, it is shameful that he is barely remembered at all.

On these pages it is hoped that we have redressed that balance to some degree, not just highlighting one of the best hurdlers not to have won the Champion itself, but, in showing the contemptuous ease in which he disposed of See You Then and company at Kempton, honouring a true great who perhaps stands at least alongside the likes of Istabraq, Persian War, Comedy of Errors and Bula in the ultimate role of honour.

SONNY SOMERS

What is the biggest difference between Flat racing and National Hunt racing?

On one side you have the mega-rich owners, happy to spend millions of pounds on an untried yearling which may have one glorious summer as a three year old before being shipped away to stud somewhere. On the other side someone with perhaps just a few thousand to invest buys some huge shaggy beast which turns out year after year with no real chance of being a sound financial investment.

Flat race jockeys earn their often quite princely sums in less than a couple of minutes on the course while their jumping counterparts sometimes just manage to scrape a living while running the very real risk of serious injury at every obstacle in their chosen profession.

Although times are slowly changing, trainers on the Flat are still generally thought of as well spoken, titled types who run state-of-the-art stables set in hundreds of well manicured acres while the Jumps trainers are still portrayed as flat-cap wearing, craggy faced types, effing and blinding their way around a maze of sheds, barns, converted coal bunkers and the like which house their horses.

Perhaps it's the enthusiasts themselves which are the biggest difference.

Compare those who stroll around Ascot dressed as if going to a ball (or fancy dress party) and know next to nothing about racing, to the true enthusiast who will stand around in the rain and cold of whatever the winter months throw at them and could probably recite the form of hundreds of horses from any year you could name.

Personally I think it comes down to love. Love of that grand old chaser, a friend whose fortunes you've followed for many years no matter what the result. You wouldn't catch anyone on the Flat backing a horse with virtually no chance of winning its race, but on the Jumps you would feel a traitor to desert one whose fortunes you've followed for many years, just in case that one day proved to be the day they came home in front.

On that note we travel back to Southwell racecourse on 4th February 1980 for a very average 3 mile chase run on heavy ground.

Two horses were heavily backed for the race, Dark Beau, whose odds had halved from their original 8/1 and the favourite, Lord Brae, trading at 100/30 after two fine runs, the last of which was when second to Turk, but Lord Brae now had a huge pull at the weights.

Turk had won four of his seven races so far this season, including the last two, and been placed in the other three so the 11/2 on offer looked rather appealing.

Trojan Walk at the same price was an out and out stayer who would relish the conditions and had also already won twice this season.

Flittermore and Silberto seemed to have very little chance and were priced accordingly but still represented the hopes and dreams of their respective owners.

At this point the field comprised a couple of eight-year-olds, three nine-year-olds and a ten year old.

Was it then the love of an old friend which had the other runner trading at 5/1? At eighteen years old (yes, 18), Fred Winter's charge, Sonny Somers, had been around longer than Methuselah. Admittedly he hadn't actually won a race since he was sixteen, in itself a feat, but he had been placed five times from as many races this season.

Always kept to around his favoured three miles, Sonny Somers had started his current, and final, campaign by making most of the running at Windsor, staying on to be an 8 length 3rd before finishing a 5 length 4th place at Leicester. At Devon and Exeter he actually led at the last fence before going down by just over 4 lengths to two much younger rivals. An eleven length third place at Kempton was then followed by another trip to Windsor where he ran his best race to be a 5 length runner up.

True enough he had a bit of form but no horse of his age had ever won a race under rules. Still, off a reasonable weight of 10 stone 8 pounds and with Fred Winter's 7 pound claimer, Ben De Haan, in the saddle he didn't lack for support.

Giving a stone to our hero, Turk made the running over the first five fences at a sensible pace with the rest of the field jumping well enough in behind. Bottom weight Flittermore then took up the running, again at a sensible pace, until they approached the thirteenth fence. At this point Sonny Somers jumped to the front while the heavily backed Dark Beau started to fade out of contention in the ground.

By the next fence both Turk and Flittermore had dropped out while Lord Brae could only stay on at one pace with Silberto starting to fade at the next.

At the head of affairs Sonny Somers was meeting every fence with the precision honed by his previous 106 races. Trojan Walk was trying to stay with him but could not accelerate as Sonny Somers started incredibly to draw clear.

As he passed the post comfortably 8 lengths clear of Trojan Walk with a further 15 lengths back to Lord Brae, Sonny Somers re-wrote history by becoming the oldest jumper ever to win a race under rules.

With 25 wins from 107 races to his eternal credit and the season drawing to a close Sonny Somers made his last appearance on Thursday 28th February at Lingfield Park, again on heavy ground over 3 miles.

On 11 stone 3 lbs he was giving weight to all bar one of his rivals but was still sent off the 9/4 joint favourite. This time Fred Winter's old charger, again with Ben De Haan in the saddle, came from behind to beat the other joint favourite by an easy five lengths, receiving rapturous applause from the crowd as he was led into the winners enclosure for the 26th and final time, a deeply loved hero to all who love racing.

WAYWARD LAD

The highs and lows of a top class steeplechaser can sometimes be extreme, but few have had the rollercoaster ride experienced by one of the most popular chasers of the 1980's, Wayward Lad.

Foaled in 1975, Wayward Lad was sold as a yearling at the Ballsbridge sales for 2,500 guineas and left to grow for a couple of years before being sent to Doncaster sales. Tony Dickinson took an instant shine to the well mannered and immensely likable gelding and bought him privately for 5,250 guineas and let him grow further before asking anything of him on a racecourse.

Flying in his work at home his debut in a novice hurdle at Leicester in 1979 was nothing more than a steering job, the stable staff making a small fortune having backed him all over Harrogate and Leeds.

With Tony Dickinson passing the training duties to his son, Michael, Wayward Lad's novice season of six wins from eight starts ended in landing the big novice event at Aintree with ease.

As a novice chaser the following season Wayward Lad was a short price for the Sun Alliance Chase at the Cheltenham Festival after a string of good results, interrupted only by unseating his jockey at Haydock last time out. Never out of the first two in all his other races, Wayward Lad ran a shocker and was unplaced, yet bounced back to win the Welsh Champion Chase a month later.

The 1981-'82 season saw Wayward Lad's star ascend the chasing ranks with incredible speed. His six wins from seven races were all achieved over 2½ miles in some of the best races around. Every series of "ups" always seem to have a "down" and the first of these came in the big Festival trial at Cheltenham over 3m1f in January where the 6/5 favourite could only finish a well beaten 3rd. Bouncing back from this he then won two more races before the rollercoaster nearly came off the rails altogether. Michael Dickinson was walking across the yard when suddenly his trusted head lad, Brian Powell, came running out of Wayward Lad's box calling, "I think Wayward's broken a leg!"

On inspection it looked horribly like it, the horse was apparently in an advanced state of shock, holding a hind foot up and shaking it frantically as if he had broken the pastern. Tense minutes passed until it was discovered the trouble was only some gravel lodged in the hoof, yet no-one knows why he reacted so badly that day. A few weeks later Wayward Lad rounded off his season by winning a second Welsh Champion Chase.

No less a trainer than David Nicholson had already pointedly advised Michael Dickinson that his horse didn't like Cheltenham and would barely get 3 miles. The following season would go a long way to refuting these arguments.

A facile victory at Worcester would then see Wayward Lad thrown into Cheltenham's two big early season handicaps, for both of which he'd start favourite. In the Mackeson Gold Cup Wayward Lad lugged 11.13 into an impressive third place behind Fifty Dollars More. In the Kennedy Construction Gold Cup a month later and carrying 12.0 Wayward Lad was a 1½ length runner up to another top class horse in Observe. In both cases he was conceding around a stone to the winner. Sixteen days later and at level weights Wayward Lad jumped the last fence in the King George level with Fifty Dollars More and the reigning champion, Silver Buck, before finding an extra gear to land the mid season crown. John Francome, who had the ride that day admitted he was "off the bridle for most of the way"; hardly surprising when you consider the pace was set by no less than Little Owl and Night Nurse. Many years later Francome confirmed that Wayward Lad was, "the most athletic horse I have ever ridden", while Fred Winter chipped in that Wayward Lad was, "the best jumper since Pendil". To cap a memorable season Wayward Lad then took third place in the Cheltenham Gold Cup amid Michael Dickinson's famous five.

Another season and another string of impressive victories included the Charlie Hall, a second Peterborough chase and a course record time in landing a second King George before the wheels fell off again in the

Cheltenham Gold Cup. Backed in to favouritism, Wayward Lad was never going well and pulled up.

In a small way Wayward Lad bounced back from this reverse by winning his opening two races of the 1984/85 season before being firmly put in his place by Burrough Hill Lad, first at Wetherby and then at Kempton in the King George. Another defeat, this time at Ayr preceded a dismal showing in the Cheltenham Gold Cup, yet with Francome back in the saddle Wayward Lad signed off with a victory in the Whitbread Gold Label Cup at Aintree.

If nothing else, the next season was to exemplify Wayward Lad's rollercoaster career to a fine degree, now under the care of Monica Dickinson after Michael's switch to the Flat. A second Charlie Hall victory was first on the agenda, quickly followed by unseating Graham Bradley at Haydock and then comprehensive defeats in Chepstow's Rehearsal Chase and the Tommy Whittle back at Haydock.

With little going right for him, Wayward Lad was allowed to drift right out to 12/1 next up in the King George, having opened at 7/1. In a fantastic race the 10 year old turned the form right around, suddenly sprouting wings in the home straight under the strongest of driving to join battle with Combs Ditch in a pulsating encounter which saw our hero win by a neck and become the first horse to win this prestigious race three times.

As if this wasn't enough excitement for one season, the Gold Cup which followed was both one of the most exciting and harrowing ever seen. Dawn Run had led for a long way, tracked by Stearsby with Wayward Lad and the reigning champion, Forgive 'n' Forget closing fast. All four approached the last fence locked together when suddenly there were three, then two as Dawn Run dropped away. Wayward Lad jumped the last fence cleanly and headed up the stamina sapping hill to glory as Forgive 'n' Forget also faded. With barely 25 yards to run Wayward Lad emptied, the extra quarter mile was just too far for him, but he gallantly tried to hang on. In a supreme effort Jonjo O'Neill galvanised the beaten Dawn Run who suddenly devoured the lead and got up close home to win in a course record time.

To watch this race it is both heartrending and impossible to believe

Wayward Lad did not win. Controversially, a 5lb mares allowance had been introduced only two years earlier and without this concession many believe Dawn Run's one length victory would not have happened. If he'd held on up the hill, Wayward Lad would have been lauded as one of the all time greats instead of just a very good one, so fickle are the fates in this game of ours.

Some years later Monica Dickinson was asked if she still had nightmares about this race, to which she replied; "Certainly not. I don't think about it. I can't bear to".

From such a fantastic two races Wayward Lad plumbed the depths again at Aintree. In a four runner race Dawn Run fell at the first only for Wayward Lad to let Beau Ranger get unassailably away from him in the back straight.

Wayward Lad's final season began with three placed efforts before another crack at the King George. The baton had now passed to a younger generation as the unconsidered Desert Orchid ground Wayward Lad and his other rivals into submission.

A poor fourth place at Ayr and a gallant fifth place behind The Thinker in the Gold Cup was bringing the story of Wayward Lad to a muted closure with just a farewell race left back at Aintree.

Regular pilot, Graham Bradley, hadn't expected his partner to be entered for the Whitbread Gold Label Cup again and had already accepted the ride on the promising Stearsby, whose jockey, Graham McCourt, had been discarded by connections. McCourt then picked up the spare ride on Wayward Lad, still an unfancied 7/1 shot despite a welter of sentimental money for the old warrior.

Without a win for over 15 months Wayward Lad turned back the clock and rose majestically to the challenge. Passing the tiring Stearsby in the home straight to the delight of Bradley, Wayward Lad bore down on the leader to take it up at the last and gallop all the way to the line, tears and cheers mixed together as he pulled seven glorious lengths clear at the line.

Twenty eight wins on sixteen different courses from 55 races and only 6 times unplaced. What a way to finish and head into honourable retirement ... or so everyone thought. Incredibly Wayward Lad had one more battle on his hands and this one he simply had to win.

Shirley Thewlis owned 60% of Wayward Lad and was more than happy for him to enjoy the retirement he now deserved. Unfortunately Les Abbott, who owned the remaining 40% was adamant that Wayward Lad should now ply his trade in low grade Hunter Chases and even point-to-points. Understandably a lot of the racing world and most race goers were horrified, but Abbott could not be dissuaded. With no resolution to the problem, Wayward Lad was consigned to be sold at Doncaster sales, nine years after he first appeared there.

Tony Dickinson was very worried about how much would be needed to ensure the horse had the retirement he so richly deserved. Shirley Thewlis made it clear that she would take none of the proceeds of the sale if Dickinson was successful, thus allowing him to increase his bidding capability.

Les Abbott had a former trainer already lined up and made his intentions very clear, all of which was widely reported in the racing press. As a result, Dickinson found himself besieged by hundreds of letters from well-wishers containing five pounds here and ten pounds there until he had a bank big enough to go to war with.

A further twist to the tale came when a certain Aiden O'Connell, a disqualified person under the rules of racing, made it plain he would outbid Dickinson and use Wayward Lad for hunting in his own County Limerick.

Michael Dickinson was training in America at this time near firm family friends Rusty and Joy Carrier who learned of the predicament and immediately contacted Tony Dickinson and pledged "whatever was needed" to win the auction through their agent, Jack Doyle, if Dickinson was forced to drop out.

On 21 May 1987, the last day of the sales, lot 600 was brought in. The place was packed as never before. It seemed the world and his wife were present along with TV and news crews. With no room available the auctioneer, a confessed fan of Wayward Lad and supporter of the Dickinson cause, allowed Tony and Monica Dickinson to stand in the ring itself, with Jack Doyle at their side in case he was needed while Wayward Lad stood placidly by, awaiting his fate.

Tony Dickinson opened the bidding at 10,000 guineas. Les Abbott topped it and battle was joined until he suddenly dropped out. For a brief moment Dickinson thought he had won but then Aiden O'Connell entered the fray. Up and up the bidding went, reaching unprecedented levels. At 42,000 guineas O'Connell shook his head, the gavel crashed down by a jubilant auctioneer, Monica threw her arms around Wayward Lad's neck and wept while the rest of the place erupted in cheering and clapping. Wayward Lad had won perhaps the most important contest of his life.

Rusty and Joy Carrier paid for Wayward Lad to be flown over to their extensive farm in Pennsylvania where he was visited regularly by Michael Dickinson. On occasions he went hunting in the widespread woodlands and meadows of the farm, showing the younger American horses a clean pair of heels with his precision jumping.

For fifteen glorious summers he had a most perfect retirement until eventually, in October of 2003, at the grand old age of 28, perhaps still remembering his extravagant leaps, the cheering of the crowds and the glories which were his, Wayward Lad was gently led from his box one last time for a pick at the grass and then quietly put to sleep.

The racing world mourned the passing of a legend.

MOSCOW FLYER

Only once in a generation in any sport does an event of such titanic proportions between supreme champions actually meet and exceed the expectations of the massed ranks who come from far and wide to witness such a battle.

Boxing had Muhammad Ali fighting Joe Frazier in the "Thriller in Manilla", Tennis had that epic Wimbledon final between Bjorn Borg and John McEnroe, Athletics had multiple world record holders Steve Ovett and Sebastian Coe going head to head at the Olympics. Every sport has its Once-in-a-Generation spectacle and for racing that moment came at Sandown Park racecourse on Saturday December 4th 2004.

The build up to this race had been several years in the making, starting at the Cheltenham Festival two seasons earlier.

At the 2003 Festival Azertyuiop put up a fantastic peformance as the 5/4 favourite, putting a breathtaking 11 lengths between himself and his nearest pursuers in the Arkle chase. On the very next day the previous year's Arkle winner, Moscow Flyer sauntered away to record a 7 length victory in the 2 mile Champion Chase as the 7/4 favourite. So, even before that years' Festival had ended, many were already anticipating a momentous clash between these two next year.

The following season Moscow Flyer and Azertyuiop met for the first time. At level weights in the Tingle Creek chase in December, Moscow Flyer justified favouritism to win by 4 lengths from a clearly unfit Azertyuiop.

At the 2004 Cheltenham Festival they had the rematch the day after a young horse called Well Chief had beaten Kicking King to win the Arkle.

In the Champion chase Moscow Flyer started at 5/6 and fell when still going well while Azertyuiop stormed up the hill in commanding style at 15/8 to record an easy 9 length victory and rightly be crowned Champion Chaser.

The Moscow Flyer camp always felt they would have won if their star had stood up, but seeing the way Azertyuiop powered up the hill that day it is hard to see how anything would have beaten him, such was his authority.

So, with a win apiece in two races where one protagonist was unfit and then the other fell, all attention was turned to Sandown Park on 4th December 2004.

This is always a popular meeting with the roads closest to the course quite congested but such was the expectation this day that the traffic jam tailed all the way back to the A3 and crawled to the course, many having to park where they could find a place and walking the last mile to the course as the time for the start of the day's entertainment fast approached. Indeed a record for the meeting of 16,300 thronged the course that day.

After a few other races the runners for the big race made their way to the parade ring. Cenkos, winner of the race in 2002 when Moscow Flyer unseated his rider by jumping into the back of another horse looked well. Upgrade and the two 300/1 outsiders Blazing Batman and Blackchurch Mist took their place while Azertyuiop strode majestically round as if he owned the place. The 10 year old Moscow Flyer approached the parade ring and stopped at the top of the hill, surveying the crowds, packed 4 deep, knowing they had come to pay homage to him and his nemesis, Azertyuiop, 3 years his junior. Both horses held an entry in the 3 mile King George VI chase as it was widely felt that this showdown would result in the loser being stepped up in distance, such was the strength of the other.

Azertyuiop, the highest rated chaser in Britain and Ireland, rated 2 lbs superior to even Best Mate. Moscow Flyer, unbeaten in the 15 chases he had stood up in, 7 of them Grade 1's, and faller in the other 5. Strangely Moscow Flyer had a perfect record of three wins and then a fall for his entire chasing career. After winning his last three races, would he continue the trend and fall today?

With this two headed monster which everyone in racing wanted to see do battle, Martin Pipe had still elected to enter his 5 year old, Well Chief, and bullishly expected him to upset the two principals after a promising pipe opener at Cheltenham where he went down by only a head. This resulted in a three way clash of the 3 most recent winners of the Arkle chase.

Moscow Flyer had limbered up with a facile 25 length victory at Navan while Azertyuiop had run away with the Haldon Gin Gold Cup at Exeter by an easy 5 lengths. The principals were fully fit and well and no prisoners would be taken today.

They paraded before the stands and cantered to the two mile start, girths were checked as they circled and waited for the starter to call them in, last minute bets were made and the buzz of excitement mounted then they lined up, the tapes rose and they were off.

Cenkos led on the inside as they all cleared the first fence safely, Moscow Flyer lying second on the outer, Azertyuiop tracking Cenkos on the inner then Upgrade and Well Chief with the two outsiders staying out of trouble at the rear.

The field jumped cleanly into the back straight and they approached the water jump in Indian file, Cenkos from Moscow Flyer, Azertyuiop then Well Chief, two lengths between each of them. At the three railway fences Richard Johnson drifted Cenkos into the middle of the course and met all three wrong. Moscow Flyer met the first in his stride then got in tight at the next while Azertyuiop and Well chief jumped quickly and accurately.

At the last of the railway fences Moscow Flyer flew it and jumped into the lead to a huge cheer from the grandstand.

Three to jump and Moscow Flyer led from the menacing figures of Ruby Walsh and Azertyuiop closing on the outside while Timmy Murphy and Well Chief took third place.

As they came to the pond fence Barry Geraghty on Moscow Flyer had a long look round at the opposition. Was this a sign of confidence before he kicked on or was it a look of concern? Moscow Flyer didn't kick on and Azrtyuiop closed down on the outside while Well Chief came under pressure.

Moscow Flyer got in tight and then Geraghty looked around again, the figure of Azertyuiop stalking him towards the penultimate fence. This time, however, as he had planned all along, Geraghty gave Moscow

Flyer a kick and away he flew.

Two out and Moscow Flyer was a length and a half ahead of Azertyuiop with Well Chief staying on well in third place. Geraghty went for a long one and Moscow Flyer broke Azertyuiop's heart. He was none too clever, having seen his rival jump it so immaculately and came under strong driving.

Up front Moscow Flyer went 7 glorious lengths clear and Geraghty rose in his stirrups to salute the deafening cheers from the stands. Well Chief ran the race of his life and only failed to overcome Azertyuiop by a short head with 25 lengths back to Cenkos, another 11 to Upgrade and then a distance to the two outsiders, fighting their own private battle.

Azertyuiop duly lined up in the King George and ran a gallant third to Kicking King before the rematch in Cheltenham's Champion Chase. On this day Azertyuiop made an horrendous mistake at the water jump and lost any chance but still ran on to take third place while the incredible Moscow Flyer fended off Well Chief by 2 lengths to reclaim his crown.

This was a great race in itself but the Tingle Creek chase on that December afternoon was the race of a lifetime for many and had exceeded the heady expectations in a way that will be talked about for many years to come.

Today Moscow Flyer takes part in show jumping events under the name of "Fred" and often completes double clear rounds, probably in very fast times too.

Azertyuiop was one of the very best 2 milers of all time but there will only ever be one Moscow Flyer.

GOLDEN MILLER

Mention the name of Golden Miller to any racing enthusiast and you can guarantee they will have heard of him as he is widely acknowledged as one of the all time greats. All will know he won five consecutive Cheltenham Gold Cups and most know he won a Grand National as well, but there it stops, so today we'll have a look at this legendary beast and a fascinating story which began even before he was born.

One day around the start of World War I in County Meath, Ireland, a weary British Officer about to be posted abroad called at the home of Laurence Gerahty, a prominent sporting farmer, leading a thoroughbred mare called Millers Pride. The officer knew he couldn't take his pride and joy to the nightmare he was heading to and persuaded Gerahty to look after the mare until his return home when he would settle what was owed. Sadly he never returned. With no-one to claim the horse and pay the dues, Gerahty kept the mare.

This is the famous story which has entered racing folklore, actually perpetuated by the connections themselves, yet it is almost certainly a myth. A truer account is that in 1914 a rich Dublin businessman, Julius Solomon, always on the lookout for investments, thought racehorse breeding was for him. At the home of farmer James Nugent, Solomon, who didn't know one end of a horse from the other, sent his chauffer to choose a broodmare. By chance he selected Millers Pride at a price of £100, who was then dispatched to Laurence Gerahty.

The outbreak of war saw a massive decline in the bloodstock market and Solomon quickly lost interest in the project, more or less abandoning the mare to Gerahty. Nothing was ever put in writing but as Gerahty paid all the bills and stud fees he was rightly listed in the General Stud Book as the breeder of Golden Miller. A very long time later Solomon realised that legally Millers Pride was still his property and for the sake of vanity and prestige, arranged for his name to supplant that of Gerahty as the listed breeder.

Over the years Gerahty successfully bred from Millers Pride, with not one stallion fee exceeded £5, yet Millers Pride produced a winning foal every time.

On 30 April 1927 she foaled a good natured bay by Gold Court. This would be her last foal as she died the following year. The un-named offspring was eventually sold as a yearling for 100 guineas.

Meanwhile, over in England, a young trainer called Arthur Basil Briscoe was starting out on his chosen career. At one point he bought a horse called May Crescent, which had been condemned by two different vets for having a bad heart, yet Briscoe won quite a number of good races with him.

In March 1930 Briscoe received a telegram from an old friend in Ireland asking if he would like to buy; "a really good looking 3 year old out of Millers Pride, price £500".
Briscoe remembered that Millers Pride had also been the dam of May Crescent so wired back; "will buy horse, forwarding cheque".

A week later the horse was offloaded at the village railway station and Briscoe sent a lad down to walk it back to the yard. At evening stables Briscoe saw his new purchase for the first time and was utterly horrified for the unbroken gelding had a coat like a huge wooly bear, was covered from head to tail in mud and was standing with his head down by his knees with no interest in his surroundings at all. Briscoe was all for sending him straight back to Ireland but eventually relented and considered it "the worst £500 I have ever spent".

Broken in very early and then turned out to grass he was placid to such an extent that he appeared to have no interest in life whatsoever. Briscoe named his horse Golden Miller, to which his head man famously commented; "What a good name for a bad horse".

On 1 September 1930 Golden Miller made his racecourse debut at Southwell where he was always behind and ran an awful race, Briscoe later confiding that he was so slovenly in his home work he expected him to be completely useless.

In an attempt to instil some life into Golden Miller, Briscoe took him hunting. The first fence was small, yet Golden Miller took it by the roots and nearly flung Briscoe out of the saddle. The next fence he went straight through, shattering the rails, and so it went on, every fence a calamity and so slow he couldn't keep up. After only a few hours Briscoe gave up, declaring; "I have never experienced a worse days mount".

On his return to the stables Golden Miller had heat in a leg and the same vets who had earlier condemned May Crescent, shook their heads and diagnosed a sprung tendon problem which would require at least 12 months rest.

At this juncture Philip Carr a good friend and owner of Briscoe's who had always liked the look of the tall bay offered Briscoe a £1000 for Golden Miller which Briscoe readily accepted, after which he made a near miraculous recovery.

On November 29 Golden Miller ran well to finish 3rd in a handicap hurdle at Newbury. After the race his jockey, Bob Lyall, enthusiastically reported; "he's one of the best I've ever ridden".

Somehow things had really clicked into place. Golden Miller's homework was now proving exceptional and less than two months later he trounced a big field in a maiden hurdle at Leicester. Six days later he was so keen in a 24 runner affair at Nottingham that he got caught up in the starting tapes and pulled a tooth out. Even losing a huge amount of ground he still won with ease.

Barely a month later the four year old made his 'chase debut back at Newbury, making an horrendous mistake at the last fence yet managing to keep upright, then making up so much lost ground he was only beaten a head on the line.

Sadly Philip Carr was seriously ill by this time and decided to sell his horses. By a strange co-incidence, Briscoe received a call at the same time enquiring about horses for Dorothy Paget, for which he told the eccentric owner he had the best chaser and the best hurdler in England in his yard and they were both for sale. So, for £12,000, Paget became the new owner of Golden Miller and his stable companion, Insurance.

December 4th 1931 saw Golden Miller contest a chase at Newbury for horses which had not won a chase before. The Miller easily accounted for Forbra, who would win the Grand National four months later. Incredibly

One of the most popular hurdlers of all time; the incomparable Sea Pigeon. Courtesy of Bernard Parkin.

The brilliant Jair Du Cochet, springheeled on his way to victory. Courtesy of Bernard Parkin.

Wayward Lad leads Forgive 'n' Forget, Run and Skip and Dawn Run with only the final hill to climb. Courtesy of Racing Post.

Martha's Son, Viking Flagship and Deep Sensation locked together over the last. Courtesy of Racing Post.

The power and majesty of Silver Buck. Courtesy of Racing Post.

Best Mate, legendary triple Gold Cup winner before his last race at Exeter. Courtesy of Graham Buddry.

Desert Orchid leads Ten Plus, Yahoo, Slalom and Charter Party in the 1989 Cheltenham Gold Cup. Courtesy of Bernard Parkin.

Golden Cygnet cruises home miles clear in the 1978 Supreme Novice Hurdle.
Courtesy of Bernard Parkin.

Jumping for fun. Sonny Somers and a very young John Francome.
Courtesy of Bernard Parkin.

an objection was lodged against the winner, not just after the race but the following day. It transpired that the horse, having won a hurdle race which hadn't been declared by Briscoe who had mistakenly mis-read the conditions of the race, Golden Miller had carried the wrong weight and was disqualified. The National Hunt Committee decreed that all bets should be settled as per the original result which was good news for both Briscoe and Paget who had placed hefty wagers on their horse. Briscoe later conceded that this was the best possible result as it left Golden Miller still eligible for maiden chases.

Second place and then a distance victory at Gatwick led to a first encounter with the Cheltenham Gold Cup. Briscoe didn't want to run this year as the fences were so exceptionally stiff that the clerk of the course was ordered to remove the top six inches of each fence by the National Hunt Committee. Paget insisted on running and after jumping the first two fences badly it became a matter of record that the five year old won by a handsome 4 lengths at odds of 13/2. Stablemate Insurance won the Champion Hurdle on the same afternoon.

The following season Golden Miller won five of his six races, including a second Gold Cup by an easy 10 lengths at odds of 4/7, Insurance again winning the Champion Hurdle for the same connections. The Miller's only defeat was at Aintree in the Grand National. Well up with the leaders after the first circuit he made a minor blunder at second Beecher's before clouting the next so hard jockey, Ted Leader, was unseated.

The 1933-34 season saw three wins from five starts. The first of these was at Lingfield at the end of November when slamming Thomond II and Kellsboro Jack when still patently unfit. A still unfit Golden Miller then narrowly failed to give Southern Hero two stone round Hurst Park while in the Gold Cup three different horses threw down serious challenges to The Miller yet by three out he had beaten them all off and sauntered home the easy 6/5 winner.

Golden Miller travelled up to Aintree by train the day before the National and was pronounced "exceptionally fit" by Briscoe as a record crowd packed the racecourse for the big event. Two horses refused to jump off and one or more fell at almost every fence on the first circuit.

From the canal turn, Golden Miller, under the welter burden of 12.2, had been in a group of five which included Thomond II and former winners Forbra and Gregalach. By Valentine's on the second circuit it was still Delaneige, who had led from the first fence, Forbra, Thomond II and Golden Miller clear of the rest. Forbra dropped back as they turned for home with Thomond II quickly following suit. At the last fence Delaneige was still there, trying for a pillar-to-post victory but his jockey was hard at work. By contrast, Golden Miller was still on the bridle and full of running, shooting clear after the last fence to win in a canter. The record time Golden Miller set for this race stood for many years until Red Rum, carrying just 10.5, lowered it in 1973 after his epic battle with Crisp.

To this day Golden Miller remains the only horse to win both the Cheltenham Gold Cup and Grand National in the same season.

Briscoe trained Golden Miller especially for the 1935 Grand National and was mortified when Thomond II was left in the Gold Cup against all expectation. The Miller was far from fit and jockey, Gerry Wilson, hadn't ridden for 10 days since badly injuring his shoulder in a fall. Wilson, in considerable pain, only took two rides at the three day meeting, winning the Champion Hurdle on the hard pulling Lion Courage before Golden Miller in the Gold Cup. Side by side all the way round Golden Miller went half a length up approaching the last only for Thomond II to put in a terrific leap to jump level, The Miller only asserting his superiority close home and thus winning his fourth Gold Cup.

There were fears that Golden Miller would be "got at" before the National so Paget employed two private detectives to stand round-the-clock watch together with four stable employees.

Despite the hard race at Cheltenham he was a public hero and they plunged on him for the National as never seen before or since. Starting the 2/1 favourite, the shortest in the race history, Golden Miller looked about to refuse at the fence after Valentine's. Booted into it by his jockey he bucked as he jumped and deposited his rider on the turf. On his return Wilson stated his mount; "didn't feel quite right". Two vets were called in to examine the horse and could find nothing amiss so Golden Miller lined up the following day for the Champion Chase. Looking fine as he cantered to post, Golden Miller unseated his rider at the very first fence.

Paget was absolutely furious, claiming Briscoe had over galloped him prior to Aintree and squarely blamed him for the defeats. Briscoe, incensed by this vitriol asked Paget to remove her horses from his stable. With neither side backing down, Golden Miller and Paget's other horses were sent to Owen Anthony.

At Newbury the following spring Golden Miller looked set to refuse at the fifth from home before veering sharply right and running out. He redeemed himself in the Gold Cup at odds of 20/21, taking up the running three out for another effortless 12 length victory, but at Aintree he unseated his rider at the first fence. Quickly remounted he continued until refusing at the same fence as the previous year. A brilliant horse over park fences, Aintree wasn't his style at all, which makes his win in 1934 even more remarkable.

There was no Gold Cup in 1937 due to atrocious weather, robbing The Miller of a sixth victory, yet Golden Miller lined up yet again the following year. Three out the favourite took it up with only his stablemate, Morse Code, able to go with him. Two out and round the final turn into the home straight and Golden Miller had a half length lead but the eleven year old was being pushed out. Morse Code was going easily on the bit and took the lead over the last only for Golden Miller to dig in and battle back, the crowd willing him on. Incredibly sound as he was, time had caught up on The Miller and second place spelt his only ever defeat around Prestbury Park, however the cheer which greeted him into the enclosures exceeded even that for the winner.

Golden Miller had winning prize money of £15,005 for his 29 wins for eight different jockeys. Not once did he fall in over 50 races running on 15 different courses under 17 different riders and was finally retired to a life of ease at Elsenham stud in West Sussex.

Briscoe, having already suffered the death of his young wife disappeared from the racing scene in 1939 and was rarely seen again. He died in 1951 aged just 48.

Dorothy Paget had great success as an owner but died of heart failure in February 1960, 12 days short of her 55th birthday.

Golden Miller had a very long and happy retirement at Elsenham with his former stablemate and lifelong friend, Insurance. On January

12th 1957 Golden Miller was put down in his box having suffered a heart attack during the night. He was 30 years old. Deprived of his friend, Insurance died just three months later.

A quiet and reserved horse he didn't have the presence of an Arkle and affording his fences the minimum daylight he didn't have the exuberance of a Desert Orchid, so others have been more popular down the years, but none can, or ever will, match his record. There will only ever be one Golden Miller.

LEVERAMOSS

When you consider just how many horses set hoof on a racecourse each year it is surprising how few there are that have their own ideas about the game regardless of what instructions their pilot gives. It's also strange that almost every one of these "lovable rogues" have more than the average helping of talent.

It's a well known fact that the great champion, Captain Christy, was as mad as a hatter, to put it mildly, but at least he consented to race, while others would just plant themselves at the start of a race and nothing short of dynamite could get them to go.

Here we will take a look at perhaps three of the biggest, yet extremely talented, rogues the game has ever seen.

Most people who have been in the game long enough will have heard of Vodkatini, primarily because his tantrums at the start were often in important races shown on television, but this wasn't initially the case.

Trained originally by Peter Haynes, Vodkatini spent three seasons hurdling with quite a number of good wins to his name and no real hint of the problems to come. If tactics had him jumping off fast and running up with the pace, Vodkatini was invariably involved in the finish while his only bad runs occurred when he was held up or ended up behind a wall of horses.

The first glimpse of a clue to his later temperament was in a novice chase at Huntingdon one December when he whipped round at the start losing ground and all but depositing his jockey on the turf. The combination stayed intact, however, and Vodkatini opened his account over the larger obstacles with ease.

The following season Vodkatini moved to the Findon stables of Josh Gifford and the subsequent years saw him develop into a high class chaser with an impressive string of victories including the 1988 Grand

Annual Chase at the Cheltenham Festival. On occasions he had been difficult at the start and Gifford or one of his staff would often be on hand to ensure he jumped off cleanly.

The Tingle Creek chase at Sandown in December 1988 was a high profile televised affair which was looked on as virtually a match between Vodkatini and Desert Orchid. Perhaps Vodkatini knew something the rest of the racing world was only just starting to realise, but as the tapes went up Vodkatini planted himself and nothing on this earth was going to make him move...needless to say Desert Orchid went on to win as he pleased.

A minor victory against modest opposition next time out was followed by a gallant third place to Desert Orchid and Kildimo in the King George VI chase at Kempton over a distance well beyond Vodkatini's best. Unfortunately this was to be the last time Vodkatini would be seen at his best.

Sent to Ascot to tackle the great grey horse again in the Victor Chandler, Vodkatini was close up when falling at the fifth fence and fell again in his next race a few weeks later before the nine year old flatly refused to race in his last outing of the season at Aintree.

The next season saw Vodkatini lose all semblance of form and become increasingly difficult, where even the occasional application of blinkers made no difference. His only placing was on his seasonal appearance when a poor second of three runners after misbehaving badly at the start. Form entry for subsequent races reads; "Mulish at start, eventually raced but pulled up after two fences" and "Unruly at start, set off well behind the rest".

A new season did little to increase his enthusiasm as Vodkatini refused to race when sent to Chepstow in October, yet two weeks later in the Charisma Gold Cup at Kempton our hero took a strong hold and set off like his former self before fading late on and finishing fourth.

Vodkatini's final season contains the uninspiring form figures, UUPPP and so the thirteen year old was retired to be remembered forever as a villain rather than the brilliant racehorse on his day he undoubtedly was.

Next up in our "Rogues Gallery" is Pukka Major.

The similarities to Vodkatini are amazing, although Pukka Major was not quite in the same league as Vodkatini over either hurdles or fences.

Originally trained by Oliver Sherwood, Pukka Major was a decent sort who won more than his fair share of races and the only glimpse of things to come was a slight reluctance to jump off at Cheltenham one day.

Pukka Major had developed into a high class sort with a string of victories before being switched to another Lambourn trainer in Tim Thomson-Jones. Further victories in increasingly better class races eventually culminated in the 1989 running of the Grand Annual Chase at the Cheltenham Festival, a year after Vodkatini had won the same event. The change of scene also saw Pukka Major become more and more difficult and again this is where the devil in the beast was seen to its worst effect.

A comfortable victory first time out the following season at Kempton was swiftly
followed by a trip to Ascot where he refused to race. Two weeks later Pukka Major was sent to Cheltenham where he reluctantly set off in no more than a canter before refusing at the first obstacle and a fortnight later virtually repeated the trick at Newbury, consenting to start only when the other runners had already disappeared over the first fence. Hopelessly tailed off, Pukka Major was pulled up at the fourth.

Another season and, again like Vodkatini, Pukka Major lost all semblance of form and his eight races yielded comments such as; "Reluctant to race", "Tailed off in rear throughout", "Always in rear. Appears to have a mind of his own now" and "Reluctant to race, tailed off, pulled up".

Most people would have given up long ago but Pukka Major returned for one last season but nothing much had changed. First time up Pukka Major was again extremely reluctant to race and was so slowly into a canter that again he refused at the first fence. A very poor fifth place in his next race was swiftly followed by another slow amble at the rear of a field before refusing at the 16th fence.

Where connections had tried to sharpen Vodkatini up with blinkers, Pukka Major's jockey turned out next time sporting spurs! To say it worked would be pushing it too far, but at least Pukka Major jumped off and stayed more or less in touch to finish fifth of the six runners.

For his final start Pukka Major seemed to remember the application of spurs last time out as he started well and led from the third to the sixth fence. Perhaps it then dawned on him that the spurs were a one-off as he suddenly downed tools when still towards the head of the field and pulled himself up before the next fence. In a final attempt to emulate Vodkatini's abysmal form figures from his last five races, Pukka Major recorded an equally appalling R0R0R.

Just like Vodkatini before him, on his day Pukka Major was a very good racehorse with a long list of victories. Considering they were both racing around the same time and at the same distances, thank heaven they never actually lined up (I won't say raced) against each other!

The surprising thing with both the scoundrels mentioned so far is that they were even allowed to carry on racing after so many aberrations, especially as their best days were so obviously behind them. The last rogue to have a look at didn't get that consideration and leaves one wondering just what he might have achieved had he put his mind properly to the task in hand.

Back in the 1977/78 and 78/79 seasons a hurdler called Leveramoss proved a real Jekyll and Hyde character. When he was good he was very, very good, winning decent races at Kempton, Newbury and Sandown among others and finishing placed in other decent events. Quite often he got it into his head that he wasn't going to run and simply refused to race at all, firmly planting himself at the start or, particularly in his latter races, starting only when the other runners had jumped off and then sulking badly many lengths behind the rest of the field, earning Timeform's infamous "squiggle" in the process.

After missing a season Leveramoss was back in the hope that he would find steeplechasing more to his liking and such were stable expectations that his first effort would be right in at the deep end against some of the best around rather than facing fellow novices.

On 30th October 1980 Leveramoss was sent to Wincanton for his first attempt over fences, starting at 100/1 due to his total inexperience and the sheer quality of the opposition, from which he was getting only 7lbs.

Jumping off in front, Leveramoss led the field to half way then stayed on well to take third place to the brilliant Fulke Walwyn trained Diamond Edge with none other than the reigning Cheltenham Gold Cup winner, Master Smudge, behind in fourth place. On the strength of this performance Leveramoss had the world at his hooves although the Sporting Life sagely concluded; "Should trot up back in novice chases, but we have our doubts".

Nine days later Leveramoss was sent to Cheltenham for a six runner novice chase with stable confidence, if not public support, behind him. Having shown what he could do against some of the best around, the seven year old flatly refused to line up with the others and when the tapes went up Leveramoss stayed exactly where he was.

In a final attempt to sweeten him up, Leveramoss returned to hurdles at Folkestone just over a week later against a dozen quite modest rivals. Yet again he planted himself at the start before deciding at the last moment that he would make a very small effort, getting further and further behind until, totally tailed off his disgruntled jockey pulled up two out. The form book bears the legend; "One to steer well clear of".

When he decided to race, Leveramoss was an extremely capable beast who still had his best years ahead but he would never get the chance. At a special Jockey Club enquiry in early 1981, Leveramoss was sensationally banned from racing.

Whether your memory of Vodkatini, Pukka Major and Leveramoss is of them at their brilliant best or of Josh Gifford jumping up and down waving his arms ineffectively at Vodkatini at Sandown or Jamie Osbourne bouncing up and down in the saddle on Pukka Major at Ascot while the other runners disappear over the first fence it doesn't matter. Love them or loathe them, these rogues and villains, and others like them, certainly make racing more interesting.

DESERT ORCHID

To National Hunt fans, Christmas is all about Boxing day and the annual pilgrimage to Kempton Park for the mid-season highlight which is the King George VI Chase.

In the mid-to-late 1980's one name alone was synonymous with this meeting and that was the legendary Desert Orchid.

Such was his overwhelming popularity that many who would never normally set foot on a racecourse made this yearly trek just to see him at the place where he was virtually unbeatable. Braving the elements year after year, huddling around the braziers trying to warm numb fingers and stamping icy feet, waiting for Desert Orchid to canter majestically to post and then come home in front ... the Christmas wish of thousands.

After three wins, to match the record of Wayward Lad, and a second in the race already to his credit, Desert Orchid returned again in 1990 as an eleven year old, fast nearing the end of his racing life.

Just a quick glance at the names of the other eight runners confirmed it was a vintage line up, yet, despite having lost both races he had run in already this season, including finishing a well beaten last of four finishers in his previous race, and drifting badly in the betting from 7/4, touching 5/2 before settling on 9/4, Desert Orchid was the favourite. The people's favourite.

Perhaps the only runner with no real chance was the rank outsider, Prize Asset, a 2 miler having his first run of the season, although he quite often won his first race each year.

Another runner more notable for his exploits over the minimum trip was Panto Prince who had recorded one of the races of the decade against Desert Orchid in Ascot's Victor Chandler Chase the previous year. Panto Prince was in excellent form this season with two wins at his favoured Wincanton before finishing 7 lengths 4th to the brilliant Pegwell

Bay in Huntingdon's two and a half mile Peterborough Chase a month earlier when giving the winner 8 pounds.

The seven year old Espy was a very good horse on his day and would go on to greater things but 33/1 summed up his chances here although he had many supporters who expected a big run.

By far the youngest horse in the field, and running for the first time in England, was Francois Doumen's five year old, The Fellow. An extremely talented horse he had already won five races at Auteuil at distances from 2m1f to 3m3f.

The 11/4 second favourite, backed in from 7/2, was the imposing 8 year old and 1988 Champion Hurdler, Celtic Shot. Unbeaten in his three races this season, The Charlie Hall, Edward Hanmer and Tommy Whittle Chases, he was at the peak of his powers. In the last of these, only two weeks earlier, he won by eight lengths, getting two pounds, from Garrison Savannah, who in March would win the Cheltenham Gold Cup by a short head from The Fellow. Back in third in the Charlie Hall, giving Celtic Shot eight pounds for 14 lengths was another King George runner, Nick The Brief, already a winner the previous season of Leopardstown's prestigious Hennessey Cognac Gold Cup, beating the mighty Carvill's Hill by 5 lengths at level weights. Indeed, Nick The Brief would win many more top races in Ireland in the years to come.

Next in the betting at 4/1 and making his seasonal debut was the Jenny Pitman trained Toby Tobias. The previous season he had won four good races before finishing second in the Cheltenham Gold Cup, with Desert Orchid 4 lengths behind him that day, before ending with a brilliant victory in the Martell Chase at Aintree. Heavily against him here though, was the fact that no horse had ever won the King George first time out.

All in all, the ageing Desert Orchid's task looked formidable yet there was one other runner, by co-incidence also eleven years old, in the field who had many astute punters clamouring for the 7/1 on offer, having surprisingly drifted from an opening price of 9/2. Sabin Du Loir boasted that he had met Desert Orchid on several occasions and never been beaten by him. Indeed, on the first of their two meeting this season, on 6th November in Devon and Exeter's top race of the year, the Plymouth

Gin Gold Cup, Sabin Du Loir had dished out a 6 length beating to Desert Orchid at level weights. The previous season he had won the Arlington Premier Chase Final at Cheltenham with the likes of Celtic Shot behind him and at the start of his career, he had won at the Cheltenham Festival over hurdles with no less than Dawn Run well held in second place.

To highlight the sheer quality of the race it is notable that all of the leading contenders had won around half of the races they had even taken part in: Desert Orchid 32 wins from 64 runs, Celtic Shot 15 wins from 30, Toby Tobias 11 from 20 and Sabin Du Loir 15 victories from 29 races.

If anyone had been in any doubt that most of the massive crowd had turned up just to see one horse, those doubts were expelled as Desert Orchid was warmly applauded into the parade ring and again as he appeared on the course while the rain continued to fall steadily.

Everyone knew that Desert Orchid liked to run his races from the front but as the tapes rose and the field headed towards the first fence it was Sabin Du Loir who led from Prize Asset as the rain stopped and the sun broke through to bathe the race in winter sunshine. Panto Prince then took third place just ahead of Desert Orchid over the third and fourth fences with The Fellow and Nick The Brief well in contention while Celtic Shot, Toby Tobias and Espy brought up the rear.

By the sixth fence and turning into the home straight, Sabin Du Loir had a comfortable 2 length lead over Desert Orchid, Panto Prince and The Fellow.

The order remained more or less the same as the crowd cheered the runners past the post and onto the final circuit, over the water jump and by the time they reached the back straight, Sabin Du Loir had built a commanding 5 length advantage over Desert Orchid, who in turn had 4 lengths to spare over The Fellow, then 2 lengths back to Nick The Brief and Toby Tobias.

With a 100% record of finishing in front of Desert Orchid and still going easily, Sabin Du Loir flew the 7th from home, but just clipped the top and pitched onto his nose as he landed, valiantly struggling to find an extra leg as Desert Orchid smartly sidestepped the falling horse and the tumbling Mark Perrett.

Nick The Brief was under the whip at the next where Desert Orchid led now by a couple of lengths from The Fellow and Toby Tobias, Espy skewing badly in fourth place as Celtic Shot started to close on the leaders.

The noise from the grandstand was deafening as Desert Orchid sprung cleanly over the fourth from home, 3 lengths clear of Toby Tobias with another 8 lengths back to the fast closing Celtic Shot and The Fellow.

The runners pounded round the home turn and into the straight for the final time, the racecourse commentary completely drowned out by the incredible roar from the crowd, many unaware of who the chasing horse was, so great the cheering.

As they approached the first in the home straight, three from home, Desert Orchid incredibly pricked his ears and started to pull clear, 4 lengths, 5 lengths, 6 lengths now between him and Toby Tobias, The Fellow running on stoutly while Celtic Shot could find no more.

Two out and Desert Orchid was 8 lengths clear, then ten lengths. Toby Tobias wasn't stopping but there was nothing more he could do.

Desert Orchid knew where he was...this was his course and his race. As the cheering reached a crescendo, Richard Dunwoody and Desert Orchid passed the winning post with 12 lengths to spare over Toby Tobias, who in turn was 5 lengths clear of The Fellow with Celtic Shot another 7 lengths further adrift as the last of the four finishers.

Understandably tired but extremely proud of himself, Desert Orchid sauntered into the winners enclosure as the Boxing day crowd clamoured to see him in his rightful place. Despite the cold and the rain all was good with the world, it was a white Christmas after all. Our hero, everybody's hero, Desert Orchid, had won again.

GOLDEN CYGNET

It is a very sad fact that for the sport we love so much some horses pay the ultimate price, often before they have achieved even a modicum of their true potential.

Fred Winter's giant Killiney was one of the most brilliant novice chasers ever seen and was clearly heading for greatness before losing his life at Ascot. The same trainer's former champion hurdler, Lanzarote, was fully expected to become a superstar of the chasing ranks when, still as a novice, he lost his life in the Cheltenham Gold Cup.

Dawn Run added the Gold Cup to her champion hurdle success after only a handful of runs over the bigger obstacles but fate took her life two races later in France.

In more recent years Gloria Victis met the same sad demise as another brilliantly rising star contesting the Gold Cup. Sadly I could go on, but despite these highly talented careers being cruelly cut short before they achieved their potential, one horse who falls into this same heartbreaking category stands clear as the brightest ever star eclipsed.

As a sparely made unbroken 3 year old gelding he came up at Goffs November sales in Ireland. A first foal from an unraced mare, whose dam was also unraced he was bought by the Irish trainer Edward O'Grady for just 980 guineas. His sire was the relative newcomer Deep Run, who would ultimately prove to be one of the best and most influential national hunt sires of all time.

Under the ownership of Raymond Rooney, the light bay with a white heart on his forehead and white streak on his muzzle began his career by winning a maiden on the flat for which he was disqualified. Two races later he signed off his four year old season by landing a maiden for amateur riders in fine style. The following year a couple of promising runs down the field had O'Grady aiming his charge at Leopardstown's big November handicap over 2 miles and an avalanche of money saw his odds tumble at a frightening rate from 20/1 to 7/2 second favourite. Inexperience may have been the deciding factor though as O'Grady's stable star finished seventh behind the short priced favourite, Mr Kildare, with another future national hunt star, Anaglog's Daughter, ahead in fifth while the top class hurdler, Monksfield, third in the betting, finished ninth.

It was as a novice hurdler in 1977-78 that O'Grady's charge would take the racing world by storm, for this likable individual who would start favourite in all his races was none other than Golden Cygnet.

Sent to Clonmel in early December, Golden Cygnet opened his account in a facile manner, following up in a similar style at Leopardstown a few weeks later. At the turn of the year Golden Cygnet was sent to Naas where he had to battle for the first time against the tough and consistent Oisin Dubh, coming home two lengths in front but having to survive a Steward's Enquiry to keep the race. A spin round Punchestown made it four wins from four with the Cheltenham Festival up next for Ireland's new darling and banker bet of the meeting.

Sponsored by Waterford Crystal, the Supreme Novices Hurdle is a veritable hothouse for future champions with previous winners including Flyingbolt, L'Escargot, Bula and Beacon Light while more recent years have seen Buck House, Browne's Gazette, Hors La Loi III and Brave Inca land the spoils among others.

In 1978 a field of 18 went to post and facing Golden Cygnet were five of the best England had to offer.

Prousto had won his only start with ease and after Cheltenham would win three of his remaining four races, defeat only coming when pitched in against Monksfield and Sea Pigeon.

Bootlaces had a win and two placed efforts to his name following a first race fall while Double Bluff had three decent wins to his credit and had been placed in all his other races.

The ultra consistent Honegger had taken a race to understand the game before running up a sequence of three wins and two second places. The remainder of his season would see another two wins and a couple of places from just four more starts.

Western Rose was another who needed a debut run under his belt before realising what was expected of him by winning next time up. Showing great courage and stamina in all his races, this was followed by just failing to get the better of the smart Kybo where the two pulled clear of the field, headed by the talented Decent Fellow before resuming winning ways in the Tolworth hurdle at Sandown. Unable to cope in bottomless ground at Chepstow, Western Rose would easily win his only start after Cheltenham.

These five among the rest of the field were expected to test Golden Cygnet to the full and ensure that whatever won deserved its place in the winners enclosure. That was the plan anyhow.

Six very good and consistent horses, but at Cheltenham only one of them was seriously backed, right in to 5/4, and these odds looked like a gift as Golden Cygnet cruised through his race, held on a tight rein by Niall Madden. Along the back straight and down the hill they flew, strung out like confetti in the wind as one after another the challengers called enough behind the hard held leader. As they powered towards the penultimate flight in this fast run race only Western Rose was still in contention, this tough, never-say-die beast whose stamina would propel him up that famous hill if he could stay with the leader long enough. At one stage it looked like a race might develop except that Golden Cygnet, still lobbing along on the bridle, was just toying with his opponent. At two out Madden let Golden Cygnet go and his acceleration was nothing short of awesome as he quickly sped clear, flew the last and cantered past the post by an untroubled 15 lengths from Western Rose. Bootlaces was a further 3 lengths back in third place, followed by Honegger, Double Bluff, Prousto and the rest of the field strung out behind.

Superlatives were still being heaped on Golden Cygnet when later that day one of the best Champion Hurdles saw a pulsating finish as Monksfield just held off Sea Pigeon, with Night Nurse third and Beacon Light back in fourth place. This fantastic race and driving finish recorded a time almost two seconds slower than Golden Cygnet's lone saunter past the winning post an hour or so earlier over the same course and distance!

A couple of weeks later Golden Cygnet went to Fairyhouse for the

Fingal hurdle and another bloodless victory, before connections decided to take their superstar away from novice company and see what he could do against the very best hurdlers in the Scottish Champion Hurdle at Ayr.

Golden Cygnet went off as 7/4 joint favourite with the champion hurdle runner up, Sea Pigeon, from whom he was receiving only one pound. The third from Cheltenham, Dual Champion Hurdler Night Nurse, was also in the field as was the Cheltenham fourth placed horse, Beacon Light, who had won Kempton's prestigious Christmas Hurdle earlier in the season.

None of this seemed to matter to Golden Cygnet who had these established stars beaten all ends up as they approached Ayr's last flight of hurdles. Night Nurse still led under strong pressure with Golden Cygnet cantering all over him and Sea Pigeon looking distinctly second best back in third place. The last flight arguably changed the picture of hurdling forever as the horse with the racing world at his feet tragically suffered a horrendous fall and was fatally injured, robbing the sport of its brightest star.

Sea Pigeon got up to beat Night Nurse but connections quickly agreed they would not have beaten Golden Cygnet had he stood up, so well was he going at the time.

At the seasons end, Timeform rated Champion Hurdler Monksfield on 177, Sea Pigeon 175 and Night Nurse 170. With six wins from as many races prior to that fateful day at Ayr, the novice Golden Cygnet received a rating of 176.

This sport we love exacts a sometimes dreadful toll on the emotions and none more so than when a horse doesn't return from battle. Sadly we will never now know how good Golden Cygnet would have been and have only the scintillating memory of his demolition job at Cheltenham to remember him by. On the evidence of what happened at Ayr before that ill-fated last flight of hurdles, we lost possibly the best we would ever see...Golden Cygnet.

BADSWORTH BOY

The second day of the Cheltenham National Hunt Festival in 1983 saw the running of the 2 mile, Queen Mother Chase, the sprinting crown of steeple chasing, which produced one of the most incredible results ever seen in a championship race.

Only six runners went to post for the race but, on paper at least, almost any one of them could win it.

Drumgora, who won the crown in 1981 and was favourite when third the following year, was an easy to back 11-1, mainly due to having had only one disappointing run so far this season, but on his day he would be easily capable of winning again.

News King, another of the previous years runners, was a strong fancy in the betting market at 5-1, having reversed earlier form with another of the days runners, Artifice, when conceding nine pounds in weight when winning the prestigious 'Tingle Creek' chase over 2 miles at Sandown Park. On his last run before the championship, however, he was outpaced on the run in here at Cheltenham by the reigning champion chaser, Rathgorman, going under by 4 lengths in receipt of only two pounds.

Artifice was the old man of the party at twelve years of age, but his form could hardly be better after the disappointing blank of the previous season. He had beaten the race favourite, Rathgorman, on the latter's seasonal debut around Sandown Park and landed the valuable Metropole Cup chase over 2 miles at Ascot before splitting Fifty Dollars More and Wayward Lad in the Mackeson Gold Cup over 2½ miles at Cheltenham. He hadn't been out of the frame in six races so far this season, winning three of them, but his last run had been some three months earlier. This wasn't generally considered to be a problem as he always produced his best when fresh and the 9-1 on offer looked remarkably generous.

The Mighty Mac was the outsider of the six runners at 20-1 due to some rather indifferent form, but he had been in second place when falling at the last fence in the race the previous year, so a sudden return to his best form could put him into the reckoning as well.

Rathgorman, the 15-8 favourite and reigning champion, had by far the most impressive set of form figures on offer. His emphatic victory in the race a year earlier, at his second attempt, was his sixth win on the trot. So far this season he hadn't finished out of the first two, with even his visits to the runner up spot being honourable defeats by short margins when conceding lumps of weight. His last race, some 2½ weeks earlier at Stratford, had been against his stable companion, Badsworth Boy. On this occasion Rathgorman went under by 12 lengths when outpaced on the run in when holding every chance at the last, but at Stratford Badsworth Boy was getting 10 pounds, whereas the championship is run at level weights.

The pair had actually met once before, at Aintree the previous season, when Rathgorman fell four fences out when cantering all over his field and Badsworth Boy fell when the race was at his mercy with just the last fence to negotiate. All in all, Rathgorman was a top class champion and would be very difficult to beat.

The eight year old Badsworth Boy's form was much harder to assess. He had fallen on his chasing debut when 4-7 favourite before winning his next three chases. It would then be 25 months of hurdling before he ran in, and won, his next three steeplechases before falling again at Aintree. This season he was unbeaten in five starts against modest opposition before his defeat of Rathgorman at Stratford. With his only chasing defeats coming when he had fallen, Badsworth Boy started at 2-1, a fraction behind his more illustrious stable companion.

As the race got under way, the 1981 champion, Drumgora, led the field a strong gallop with the others tightly bunched behind and only The Mighty Mac starting to lose contention. Badsworth Boy took over the lead five fences out, far out jumping Drumgora, who now beat a hasty retreat, a light perhaps of former days. Old Artifice, too, was finding the pace far too hot and began to lose his place while out in front Badsworth Boy kept up a relentless gallop.

Rathgorman, the reigning champion, had been nicely held up until now, but suddenly, four fences from home he, too, came under strong pressure and could find little response to the leader's incredible speed and agility.

News King, the only one left to offer a challenge, came under pressure three fences out before blundering badly at the next and eventually being passed by the renewed challenge of Artifice after the last fence.

Out in front, thoroughly enjoying himself, Badsworth Boy was jumping superbly at a terrific speed, making his only mistake at the second last, to draw further and further away from a high class field struggling vainly in his imperious wake. Badsworth Boy's official winning margin was a distance ahead of Artifice and a further 6 lengths back to News King in a tired third place.

Never before and almost certainly never again would the 2 mile championship be won with such consummate ease. It was far more likely, especially considering the fast time of the race, that Badsworth Boy had proved to be something extra special, rather than all of the opposition having an off day at the same time.

Artifice returned the following year to be a 20 length 3rd to Badsworth Boy in the second of the undisputed champion's three unequalled triumphs in the race and, indeed, barring falls it would be well into Badsworth Boy's veteran years before any horse ever beat him in a 2 mile steeplechase.

Despite suffering from the debilitating navicular disease as a two year old, Badsworth Boy lived a long retirement at his owner, Doug Armitage's home near Rotherham, before succumbing to a heart attack at the grand old age of 27.

People think of Golden Miller, Arkle and Desert Orchid when talking of the racing greats simply because these horses ran over the classic, Gold Cup, distance, but, pound for pound, was there ever a horse greater than Badsworth Boy? On that glorious March afternoon a championship race was won by a distance. We had seen a class field taken apart and smashed into the ground by the best at his very best.

SPANISH STEPS

National Hunt racing has always had a romanticism about it which few other sports can ever come close to.

Who can honestly say they weren't emotionally touched when The Pie won the Grand National with a young Elizabeth Taylor in National Velvet? Velvet Brown and The Pie may have been fictitious but how equally unbelievable was it that a well built Welsh Dairy farmer could ride his own bred and owned horse in most of it's work and then send it out to beat the legendary Desert Orchid in the Cheltenham Gold Cup, yet Sirrell Griffiths did exactly that in 1990 with Norton's Coin.

Perhaps one of the most amazing stories though is that of Edward Courage, who was far from a one horse or one race wonder.

Born in 1906 and educated at Eton where he was a promising athlete, Courage was also a top rider for the Warwickshire Yeomanry in the point-to-point field. On the business front, Courage was a director of the National Provincial Bank as well as the family brewing firm when he wasn't indulging his favourite pastimes of shooting and fishing. Indeed Courage was on a fishing holiday in Scotland in 1938 when he contracted polio with the nearest hospital being Aberdeen, 70 miles away by road. The doctor's parting words to the driver about to convey Courage there were; "Don't expect him to still be alive when you get there".

A long spell in hospital ensued but Courage did survive, although he would be confined to a wheelchair for the rest of his life, his extremely active lifestyle now a thing of the past. Eight years later, to fill the void, he bought a mare called Drumrora from a cousin for £250 and began dabbling in point-to-points.

Drumrora was descended from the 1903 Grand National winner Drumcree, a half brother to two other National winners and whose daughters would themselves produce two more Grand National winners. This love of Aintree was an astounding family trait, which would be carried on down the generations.

Over the following years Courage built a small breeding dynasty based on Drumrora and her daughters and successfully applied for a permit to train and race under rules. Edward's wife, Hermione, acted as secretary and made the entries while top horseman, Jack Morgan, was employed to prepare the horses and was ultimately responsible for much of the stable's success over the years.

In their first season, 1953/54, Drumrora's two daughters, Tiberina and Tiberetta, won seven races for the stable, including four in 9 days over the Christmas period.

Within a few years Tiberetta had carried on the family tradition and shown her own love of the big Aintree fences by winning the Christmas Dinner Chase, Beecher Chase and Grand Sefton. In her first attempt at the Grand National her fast finishing run was left too late and she came third. The following year Tiberetta was inconvenienced by the heavy overnight rain but still ran well for second place and took fourth spot a year later to rightly be dubbed the "Queen of Aintree". In later years Tiberetta's son, Lictor, would win the Topham Trophy, and six other descendants of Drumrora were considered good enough to contest the National, Tiberina's great grandson, Red Marauder, landing the big race in 2001, but that lay a little while ahead yet.

As Tiberetta, who never fell in 68 races, and her sisters reached the end of their racing lives, Courage made plans with regard to their breeding program. Taking advice from his friend, John Hislop, who bred and owned the great Brigadier Gerard, Courage settled on Flush Royal.

As a three year old Flush Royal beat the subsequent Derby winner, My Love, and later took third place in the French Derby. Fifty five career races produced 18 victories, including a Cesarewitch and 23 placed efforts. Courage would send his daughters of Drumrora to Flush Royal on five occasions, for which the resultant offspring would ultimately win 54 races. Other than for the Courage stable Flush Royal would sire horses placed in several Champion Hurdles and Grand Nationals.

One of the matings between Tiberetta and Flush Royal would put Courage firmly on the map with one of the toughest, best and most popular chasers of the era. On Sunday March 24th 1963 Tiberetta brought into the world a dark bay colt who would be named "Spanish Steps".

Jack Morgan's brother, Tom, broke in most of the Courage horses and remembers Spanish Steps as being very wilful and who would often drop his riders on the gallops by bucking or whipping round. Tom Morgan also remembers him as being; "a quick learner with great big feet and an excellent jumper…a real natural like Tiberetta".

In October 1966 Spanish Steps made his racecourse debut in a 2 mile novice hurdle at Chepstow, ridden by the stable jockey, John Buckingham, who Jack Morgan had taught to ride. On heavy going after persistent rain and in a swirling fog Spanish Steps ran a creditable fourth place. Upped in class he then took second places at Newbury and Ascot before opening his account at Wolverhampton. In the nine races of his debut season this was Spanish Step's only win yet a fifth place was his lowest placing, having earlier finished third to another promising novice called Persian War.

At the end of the season John Buckingham won his 12th race of the season when Foinavon avoided the mass carnage ahead of him to win the Grand National. Many years later Buckingham recalled this season with poignancy; "If someone had asked me before Spanish Steps had ever run over fences, would I rather ride a Grand National winner or Spanish Steps in all his races, I'd have chosen the latter".

For his second season, Spanish Steps ran second on his seasonal debut before winning a race at Kempton. This earned him another crack at Persian War in the Lansdown hurdle at Cheltenham. In atrocious conditions which were so wet and heavy they were barely raceable Spanish Steps set out to make his stamina, love of the conditions and better jumping tell. Courage and Morgan both thought Persian War was a bit suspect in his jumping and planned to test their theory in the closing stages. As such, with the race between them three out, Spanish Steps led Persian War by a half length and when Spanish Steps took off, so did Persian War and was lucky to remain upright after demolishing the flight. At the next it seemed the same was about to happen but Persian War put down instead, slipped on take off and fell just the same, leaving Spanish Steps to ping the last and saunter home alone.

Edward Courage and everyone connected with Edgcote stables had realised, to varying degrees, that they had a very special horse on their hands who would be far better when put to the bigger obstacles, so, for the remainder of the season, his appearances in races such as the Schweppes and Scottish Champion hurdle were more for experience than any real hopes of victory.

The following season saw Spanish Steps put to fences for the first time, winning at the first time of asking under John Buckingham at Sandown. Two weeks later, again at Sandown, Spanish Steps was well in command with the race won rounding the home turn but an over confident Buckingham let his mount drift away from the rails and start to idle. As a consequence he failed to see an unfancied debutant staying on dourly and taking advantage of the gap on the rails to steal the race by a half length. Edward Courage took the defeat on the chin but reasoned a stronger jockey was needed: Buckingham would ride Spanish Steps only once more.

The five year old was next aimed at Ascot's newest race, the Black and White Gold Cup with new jockey John Cook. The Berkshire course had seen incessant rain for nearly a week and the heavy ground was ideal for the 10/1 shot who delighted Courage by winning with ease. Despite seemingly abundant stamina, Spanish Steps had done virtually all his racing over 2 miles, including all his chases. With the Cheltenham Festival fast approaching Courage mulled over his options as Spanish Steps held entries in both the big novice chases.

Continuous rain and heavy ground had caused the abandonment of dozens of meetings in the weeks prior to Cheltenham, which already listed the going as "heavy" with more rain forecast. Courage reasoned that the 2 mile Arkle chase on the third day may be lost to the weather, so opted for the Tote novice chase over 3¼ miles on the opening day.

A field of 22 started the Tote novice chase, run in persistent rain, which saw horse after horse fall or be pulled up while Spanish Steps relished the conditions. A brilliant jump 3 out saw off all but two of the remaining challengers and even they were well beaten before Spanish Steps flew the last and sauntered up the hill 15 easy lengths to the good. Courage had landed the big novice staying chase while later on Pride of

Kentucky won the Kim Muir and Royal Relief, another son of Flush Royal, finished a neck second in the County hurdle after demolishing the last flight...not bad for a stable of just eight horses.

In 1969, after a seasonal pipe opener, Spanish Steps lined up for the 15 runner Hennessy Gold Cup at Newbury for which the 4/1 favourite was last season's Whitbread winner, Larbawn, set to carry 12st 3lbs. Carrying a top weight of 2 pounds more was 7/1 shot Playlord, whose four victories in the previous campaign included the Great Yorkshire and Scottish National. Spanish Steps was allotted 11st 8lbs and grouped at 7/1 along with the ten stone bottom weight, Lord Jim, who had taken 3rd place, 18 lengths behind Spanish Steps, in the Tote novice chase at Cheltenham. Half a point longer in the betting and sharing bottom weight was Winsome Win, already a winner of her only four races this term.

On his favoured firm ground, Larbawn set off in front and was still there as they approached the notorious cross fence on the final circuit. Lady Mynd was a length behind on his inner with Cottager the same distance behind on Larbawn's outer. These three were closely followed by Spanish Steps, going well within himself, then Playlord, Limeburner and Lord Jim together. Larbawn jumped well but Lady Mynd and Cottager both fell independently right in front of Spanish Steps and the chasing pack. Lady Mynd rolled to the left and brought down Playlord, Cottager rolled to the right and brought down Limeburner while a fortunate Spanish Steps landed in the gap the two fallers had just vacated. In the home straight Spanish Steps powered up to Larbawn, jumped to the front at the next then pulled further and further clear over the remaining obstacles to beat Larbawn by a comfortable 15 lengths with Lord Jim in 3rd and Winsome Win running on well to take fourth place.

Just two days after Edward Courage had received the 1968/69 National Hunt Trainer of the Year award Spanish Steps had won one of the most prestigious races in the calendar on ground considered too firm for him in a time nearly 2 seconds faster than Mandarin's previous course record time, the first of two course records Spanish Steps would set at Newbury. To cap it all, this was Courage's 100th winner since taking out a permit in 1953 and the prize money lifted him to top of the Owners' table.

Spanish Steps next won Sandown's 3 mile Benson and Hedges Gold Cup, bypassed the King George as Kempton did not suit his style of running then limbered up for the Cheltenham Gold Cup by trouncing top class rivals in the Gainsborough chase back at Sandown.

Everything seemed to be right for Spanish Steps to claim chasing's crown: the course, the distance, the going, Courage was in good form as his Royal Relief was just pipped at the post in the 2 mile Champion chase. If Spanish Steps had travelled to the course the day before few doubt he would have won. Instead a local builder near his stable had a cement mixer going for hours on end and barking dogs did the rest to upset the horse who nervously walked his box for hours in a raging sweat, Morgan having to change his sweat drenched rug on three occasions.

When Cook was legged up in the parade ring Spanish Steps immediately bucked him off again while in the race he appeared lifeless, getting reminders with a circuit to go with only sheer guts enabling him to plug on into a 10 length third place behind L'Escargot.

At the end of the season Courage's nine inmates had ensured he finished as leading Owner and Breeder and finished an incredible seventh on the Trainers list – as a permit holder. For his part Flush Royal ended eighth in the leading sires list.

Another season saw further success for Spanish Steps and again he was strongly fancied for the Cheltenham Gold Cup before the cruellest of fates intervened. Making the final declarations just days before the start of the Festival, Mrs Courage inadvertently declared the stable's Trajan for the Gold Cup, in which he wasn't even entered, as well as the Mildmay, his intended target. The recording confirmed Spanish Steps had not been mentioned and racings rulers refused to accept the error and let him run. On bottomless ground he surely would have gone close.

Royal Relief managed 3rd place in the 2 mile Champion Chase while later on John Buckingham's career came to an end following a badly broken leg. John Cook had some consolation when winning the Grand National, but years later opined; "Without a doubt I got more satisfaction winning good races on Spanish Steps than winning the National on Specify".

In the next couple of years Spanish Steps won the S.G.B. chase at Ascot, was a half length second to The Dikler, who was receiving seven pounds, in the King George VI chase at Kempton and ran sixth in two more Cheltenham Gold Cups before turning his attention to the family tradition that is the Grand National. His half brother, Royal Relief, would prove his own worth by winning the 2 mile Champion Chase in both 1972 and '74 as well as a second place in the intervening year.

So, in 1973, Spanish Steps took his place in what would prove to be one of the most famous races of all time. Carrying 11st 13lbs and giving 22lbs to the winner, Spanish Steps finished a gallant fourth behind Red Rum, Crisp and L'Escargot, all four horses beating Golden Miller's long standing course record!

The following year Spanish Steps still had 11st 9lbs to lug around Aintree for another admirable fourth place behind Red Rum, L'Escargot and Charles Dickens.

The handicapper relented at last in 1975, giving Spanish Steps only 10st 3lbs but although he surged past The Dikler on the run in he had to settle for third place behind, you guessed it, L'Escargot and Red Rum again.

Retirement for the old campaigner had been briefly considered and dismissed, for as Courage said; "He wouldn't know what parish to stop in if he was hunted". So he stayed in training for one last season, of which the 1976 Grand National would prove to be 13 year old Spanish Steps' last race. During the season Spanish Steps won his last race to great applause from the crowd. Several weeks later his cancer stricken 28 year old mother, Tiberetta and her frail year older sister, Tiberina, were led out at Edgcote for the last time and put down together. Tiberetta and Tiberina won 15 races between them for Courage while their offspring added another 88 victories for the stable. They were buried together on the grassy slope behind Edgcote church.

At Aintree, with just 10 st 2lbs on his back Spanish Steps was leading or disputing the lead from before The Chair to Beecher's Brook. Here Golden Rapper fell and cannoned into Spanish Steps, badly damaging a tendon. Bravely the horse continued, his jockey, Jeff King, unaware of the problem, to finish 9th of the 32 runners behind Rag Trade and Red Rum. King had trouble pulling the old warrior up…perhaps he knew that when he stopped this time, life would never be the same again.

Drumrora had been the cornerstone of Courage's world in that 29 of her progeny went on to win Courage 152 races. Spanish Steps ran 78 times, winning 16 races and being placed on no less than 40 occasions.

Edward Courage, who died on July 3rd 1982, will be remembered for the exploits of Tiberetta and Royal Relief, but most of all for a horse called Spanish Steps.

COMEDY OF ERRORS

The Fifth Regiment first saw action in the Third Dutch War in 1674. Two hundred and ninety five years later, Newcastle racecourse set up a valuable hurdle race in honour of their nickname, "The Fighting Fifth".

Within 4 short years the race was quickly established as arguably the most important race outside of the Champion Hurdle itself and in a period of 10 years it was won by Comedy of Errors 3 times, Night Nurse, Birds Nest 3 times, Sea Pigeon twice and Ekbalco.

While Night Nurse and Sea Pigeon are rightly lauded as great champions from that golden age of hurdling and Birds Nest is acclaimed as the best hurdler never to be crowned champion, having the misfortune to be around in the same era, what of Comedy of Errors?

Foaled in 1967, Comedy of Errors was trained for the flat by Tom Corrie. By the sprinter, Goldhill, Comedy won 4 races including the Edinburgh Gold Cup.

Around this time Ted Wheatley, owner of the Allied Carpets chain, wanted to buy a present for his business partner, Harold Plotnek. Acting on his behalf, trainer Fred Rimell paid £12,000 for Comedy of Errors and so impressed was he that Rimell persuaded Wheatley to retain a half share, thus keeping the horse at Kinnersley, near Worcester.

His dam, Comedy Actress, had already produced some good National Hunt types and the breeder, Elizabeth Sykes recalls; "As a yearling Comedy of Errors went straight over a big thorn hedge to join some fillies on the other side".

As a five-year-old Comedy of Errors took his first steps on a racecourse, winning very easily on four occasions and finishing second the other twice.

The following season Comedy of Errors lined up for the first time in the Fighting Fifth, ridden by new stable jockey Bill Smith. Being stoked up for his customary finish where the huge stride of this giant of a horse literally pounds the opposition into submission, Comedy stormed 6 lengths clear of the useful Easby Abbey.

After finishing behind the reigning champion, Bula, and Canasta Lad in the Cheltenham Trial hurdle (later re-named the Bula hurdle in honour of that outstanding horse) he travelled to Ireland for the Sweeps hurdle. Beating Bula on this occasion he still managed only second place as the concession of four pounds to the enigmatic Captain Christy proved just too much.

All three horses won their prep races prior to the Champion Hurdle where Bula started the 5/6 favourite and Captain Christy at 85/40.

Fred Rimell had said to Bill Smith just before the race; "just do your best and don't fuss if he's not good enough to win". Smith, however, was full of confidence aboard the 8/1 shot and stalked the long time leader, Easby Abbey, until unleashing his challenge and winning in commanding style, Easby Abbey second, just ahead of Captain Christy with Bula fifth.

Connections of Bula were astounded and took on Comedy of Errors again in the Welsh Champion hurdle where Bula was in receipt of 6lbs. Comedy of Errors won again by a cosy 4 lengths.

In 1973 Comedy of Errors again took the Fighting Fifth en route to Cheltenham to defend his hurdling crown.

Bula and Captain Christy had switched to fences while last season's runner up, Easby Abbey, had finished only 3rd in the Fighting Fifth but it was another of the Uplands residents who had taken the mantle as standard bearer for the stable's hurdling aspirations, Lord Howard de Walden's Lanzarote.

Described by legendary trainer Fred Winter as; "Without doubt the best horse I've ever trained", this was some praise.

The long striding Comedy of Errors was far better when held up for a late challenge but, like many horses of his size, he took an age to be wound up for that challenge and as he had a tendency to hang right handed when under pressure, left handed Cheltenham was not to his liking.

Richard Pitman and Lanzarote, who preferred right handed tracks himself and was unbeaten in 8 starts around Kempton, formulated a plan to run Comedy of Errors off his feet. Bill Smith maintains that Comedy wasn't himself that day as his late challenge petered out and he finished 3 lengths second to Lanzarote.

1974 saw Comedy of Errors back at Newcastle as race favourite for the third time and odds on for the second consecutive year. The main danger appeared to be commentator Peter O'Sullivan's classy Triumph hurdle winner, Attivo, a very nippy sort who was clearly proved the best of his generation when storming up the Cheltenham hill the previous March.

With Bill Smith now moved to Fulke Walwyn's yard, Ken White had the Rimell mounts and no matter how much Attivo tried, and he tried very hard, Comedy of Errors was at his peak and dismissed his younger rival with relative ease.

Another successful campaign culminated again in the Champion hurdle where Lanzarote adopted exactly the same tactics which won him the crown the previous year. A relentless gallop from the outset had Pitman smiling until he looked over his shoulder at the top of the hill and saw the menacing shape of Comedy of Errors lobbing along in behind him. Coming down the hill Pitman started to push and shove on Lanzarote while Ken White stoked up Comedy of Errors who lengthened his stride and simply flew past his rival to win as he pleased in the heavy going.

In the history of the Champion hurdle, Comedy of Errors remains the only horse ever to regain the crown.

Comedy of Errors raced on the following season but in the Fighting Fifth he failed by 2½ lengths to give half a stone to the new superstar, Night Nurse.

By the end of the season Night Nurse was the Champion hurdler, neither Comedy of Errors or Lanzarote having enough left with the advancing years to fend off the new generation.

Comedy of Errors ran in one steeplechase, finishing second, but clearly did not enjoy the larger obstacles, so, with a National Hunt prize money record to his name he retired to enjoy the rest of his days as Mercy Rimell's hack.

In his three seasons at the top only 4 horses, Bula, Canasta Lad,

Captain Christy and Lanzarote, ever managed to beat Comedy of Errors in any race other than his customary pipe opener at Newbury.

Fred Winter, with all the exceptional horses under his care had maintained that Lanzarote was the best of the lot. Stable jockey, Richard Pitman, declares; "The truth was that Lanzarote was not quite as good as Comedy of Errors".

When talk turns to the best hurdlers, past and present, the colossus that was Comedy of Errors stands proudly towards the peak.

BARNBROOK AGAIN

As soon as one Cheltenham Festival draws to a close the National Hunt faithful are already looking excitedly ahead to the next one and while the Gold Cup itself is the pinnacle of the season, many consider the Queen Mother two mile Champion Chase as the top race to see.

The Gold Cup occasionally throws up a winner which raises a few eyebrows as just the best equipped horse on the day under the prevailing conditions while the Champion Chase invariably produces the race of the meeting and is always won by a true champion. Wednesday 14th March 1990 was no exception.

Nine horses went to post for what was to become one of the races of the season and while decent horses such as former dual champion, Pearlyman, Panto Prince and Ireland's Feroda had their supporters, it was three other horses which dominated the race.

At the head of the betting market, at a heavily backed 11/10, was the reigning champion, Barnbrook Again whose victory in the race last season, as the 7/4 favourite, gave him a perfect four wins from as many starts. Earlier he had won the Haldon Gold Cup at Devon and Exeter and the two and a half mile Arlington Premier Series Chase Final.

This season he had started by breaking Newbury's 2 mile course record when giving nearly two stone to all the other runners, followed this with a gallant 3rd place in Cheltenham's A F Budge Gold Cup over two and a half miles, again giving nearly two stone to the 1st and 2nd horses and then competed in Kempton's 3 mile King George on Boxing Day where only his stablemate, Desert Orchid, managed to beat him. His prep race for the Festival was again over 3 miles in Newbury's Compton Chase where, an hour after Feroda had won the Game Spirit Chase as an odds on favourite, Barnbrook Again sauntered home a distance clear of his nearest challenger.

Next in the betting at 4/1 was the Martin Pipe trained Sabin Du Loir who had been running solely over two and a half miles all season, winning the last three of his four outings. The most recent of these was the Arlington Premier Series Chase Final where he had won comfortably from Celtic Shot with Waterloo Boy a well trounced third.

Waterloo Boy had also strangely been campaigned solely at two and a half miles this season, never finishing out of the frame although his best effort at a distance too far for him was in beating Celtic Shot by a neck at Chepstow when giving him 7 pounds.

The previous season, campaigned at 2 miles, Waterloo Boy won 6 of his 7 races, finishing second to Sabin Du Loir at Ascot before beating him into 3rd place in the Arkle Chase at the Cheltenham Festival.

Pearlyman had two very average runs to his name this season after being out for over a year, but the 1987 and '88 Champion Chaser was a different prospect around Cheltenham and many expected him to be a leading player on the climb to the finishing post.

On good ground the pace was fast from the outset with Panto Prince leading over the first couple of fences before Sabin Du Loir went into the lead approaching the third, Barnbrook Again tucked away in 4th place and Waterloo Boy tracking him.

The order stayed much the same except for Private Views racing to the front once in a while and then either making a mistake at a fence or trying to stop as they rounded the bend away from the stands.

At the first of the ditches it was still Sabin Du Loir, Barnbrook Again and Waterloo Boy, the 500/1 outsider Impertain and the smooth figure of Pearlyman cruising into contention. At the next ditch Impertain made a bad mistake, leaving just the big four at the head of affairs, over the next and racing down the hill.

Sabin Du Loir, Barnbrook Again, Waterloo Boy and Pearlyman, all going at a cracking pace, leaving the rest of the field behind and all going well within themselves. Over the next, all foot perfect, Pearlyman jumping up into 3rd place, just starting to make his play, but something was wrong ... Pearlyman had gone lame and Tom Morgan had no option but to pull the old warrior up.

Racing down to two out and Barnbrook Again had joined Sabin Du

Loir, Waterloo Boy just behind in third, all starting to be ridden for the glory and prize which awaited. Round the home turn, the crowd roaring as only a Cheltenham festival crowd can and Barnbrook Again, the reigning Champion had forced himself half a length in front of Sabin Du Loir with the same distance back to Waterloo Boy.

On the run to the final fence and all three are locked together again, one fence and the final hill all that's left of the race and Waterloo Boy comes through to jump the last a neck in front of Barnbrook Again with only another neck separating Sabin Du Loir.

Up that final, stamina sapping hill, Peter Scudamore can find no more on Sabin Du Loir as he weakens to be eventually headed by Tom Taaffe on Feroda. At the head of things Hywel Davies and Richard Dunwoody are riding like men possessed, giving their all, their gallant partners responding again and again to every urge, every crack of the whip, stretching their necks out, striving for the line. As brilliant as Waterloo Boy is he cannot quite match the brilliant toughness of Barnbrook Again and it is he who forges on by a mere half a length to retain his crown.

Once more the 2 mile Championship had thrown up the race of the meeting, even if the hard driven finish had the shine taken off it by the stewards imposing a ban on both jockeys for the strength of their finish.

Less than a month later, back to two and a half miles around Cheltenham, Barnbrook Again absolutely trounced Pegwell Bay, Sabin Du Loir and all the others in another course record time. A super tough horse or what?

Whenever 2 milers are mentioned down the years you can be assured that Waterloo Boy will always be considered as one of the best never to have quite claimed the crown while Barnbrook Again is rightly hailed as one of the very best. In 1990 they conspired to give us a race that will live in the memory for many, many years.

BARACOUDA

The long distance hurdlers have always been considered far inferior to the championship winning two milers whose names slip off the tongue with such fluency. Indeed the winner of the Stayers' Hurdle at the Cheltenham Festival was rarely even given much more than a nod of recognition and more often than not the winner was considered barely better than a good staying handicapper. In more recent times, however, the likes of Inglis Drever and Big Bucks have given this division as a whole a much higher profile as they themselves became much loved superstars in the hurdling ranks. Nowadays The World Hurdle, as it is now known, is an eagerly anticipated event come March and a highly respected feature race of the Festival.

One horse, though, was primarily responsible for putting the staying hurdler category firmly on the map and elevating it to the respected position it holds today.

Although far better known for his many successful assaults on our top steeplechases, French maestro Francois Doumen uncovered a hurdler of such truly exceptional talent in Baracouda he would change the status of this division for ever.

Baracouda was a four year old before he contested the first of his seven runs on the flat under the care of Madame Mathis. Although kept to the more provincial tracks and never finishing worse than fifth, Baracouda never managed to get his head in front where it mattered most.

His trainer, realising he may have more presence over hurdles sent her charge to Auteuil on 26 March 2000 where again he finished in fifth place.

Roger Barby, his owner, decided on a switch to the well appointed and incredibly peaceful stables of Francois Doumen, where he would spend the rest of his racing career.

Only four weeks later back at Auteuil and under the trainer's son, Thierry, Baracouda finished second of 16 runners, beaten less than a length over a distance of just over 17 furlongs. In the next couple of months at the same course Baracouda opened his account with an emphatic win before following up in the prestigious Prix Dawn Run. These were the first of twenty five consecutive races where Baracouda would not be out of the first two, winning eighteen of them.

English racegoers had their first look at the strapping 5 year old gelding at Ascot on 16 December 2000 in the 3m1f Long Walk Hurdle.

The heavy ground was ideal for the French raider who started at 11/4 more because of the reputation of his trainer, who was renowned for his raiding parties in this country.

Seven of the other eight runners were relatively ignored in the betting as punters latched on to Martin Pipe's enigmatic Deano's Beeno under AP McCoy. The favourite was fresh from the Long Distance Hurdle at Newbury where he put an easy 17 lengths between himself and his nearest persuer.

At Ascot, Deano's Beeno led the field at a steady pace in the testing conditions with Baracouda held up off the pace. With just four flights left to jump, Deano's Beeno perceptively quickened the pace yet was quickly joined by Baracouda, going with ominous ease. McCoy got hard at work on the favourite before the next and kept the lead under strong driving until they lined up for the penultimate flight. Here Baracouda swept into the lead with no apparent effort as still on the bit he pinged the hurdle and started to pull further and further clear. Deano's Beeno was as game as they come but he simply had no chance against such a monster who ran on strongly to win by an impressive 14 lengths.

Next time out Deano's Beeno franked the form by cantering to an emphatic 30 length victory in a grade 2 hurdle at Doncaster, but by now Baracouda had changed hands. Roger Barby has had a few horses in training on both sides of the channel for quite a number of years with only modest success. This was by far the best horse he had ever owned but Baracouda had been brought to the attention of the prolific owner and gambler, JP McManus, who, as the saying goes, made him an offer he couldn't refuse.

The Long Walk Hurdle was the second of eight successive victories before a first visit to the magnificent spectacle of the Cheltenham Festival for the Stayers' Hurdle of 2002.

A large field of 16 faced the starter, for which Baracouda was the 13/8 favourite. Held up way off the pace by Thierry Doumen, which in itself made betting guru, John McCrirrick apoplectic, Baracouda was asked to steadily close on the leaders as they swept down the hill for the final time. A good jump at the last propelled the resolute galloper past his opponents where he was pushed out to win cleverly by just a neck, although he would have found far more if any of his rivals were able to mount a serious challenge. So, here at last, was the moment when the long distance hurdling championship went from being just another race at jumpings Olympics to the dawn of a new era where the winner was acclaimed as a true great.

A year later and the reigning champion was back, but this time the opposition was far tougher.

The Irish rightly love their racing and a special horse of immense ability had been taken to their collective heart. Since winning his maiden hurdle only a month short of five years earlier, Limestone Lad had only once finished outside the first four and that was in the Irish Cesarewitch on the flat! In that time he had raced against the best around and counted victories against Istabraq and Doran's Pride amongst his 29 hurdle successes. (Limestone Lad also won four of his six steeplechases). Cheltenham would be the final racecourse appearance for the eleven year old.

Opinion was firmly divided down the middle. The head may say Baracouda but the heart said Limestone Lad and in a way it was only right they shared favouritism at 9/4.

The only other one of the eleven runners seriously backed was the Jonjo O'Neill trained six year old, Iris's Gift at 7/1, who had won all five of his races over hurdles, after landing three of his five outings in Bumpers. It was these three which dominated the race from the off.

Limestone Lad, although better at slightly shorter distances, took the field along at a strong gallop which he intended to keep until the winning post. Iris's Gift ran close up in the leading three or four while

Tierry Doumen settled Baracouda right at the back of the field as usual and this was how they remained until around half way when Baracouda started making ominous progress through the field while Iris's Gift closed on Limestone Lad at the same time. With just two left to jump Iris's Gift threw down a challenge to the long time leader with Baracouda sitting just behind the pair and going so easily. Between the last two the French raider was given the signal and surged into the lead, Iris's Gift trying to go with him whereas Limestone Lad was unable to find any more. Over the last and on the run to the line Iris's Gift was giving everything he had but was always being held by Baracouda, driven hard by Thierry Doumen was responding gamely to win by three quarters of a length with a further five back to Limestone Lad.

At this time it seemed impossible that Baracouda could ever be beaten, yet there was a growing clamour to see the eight year old race over fences. Without a doubt he had the size and scope for it and would undeniably have been a force to be reckoned with over the larger obstacles, yet Francois Doumen had no intention of sending his star hurdler chasing, arguing that he was the best at what he did so why change it. When quizzed at his laid back training regime with Baracouda through the forests surrounding Chantilly, Doumen confided; "The less work he did the better he was".

In a way the trainer was right as another unbeaten run saw him attempt to land the Cheltenham prize for a record third time. In a brave attempt on ground not wholly to his liking Baracouda went down with all guns blazing. Iris's Gift had been pushed a couple of lengths clear before the last flight but Baracouda closed him down on the run to the line and for a brief moment it looked as though history would be made. As brave as he undoubtedly was, Baracouda couldn't answer Iris's Gift's final driving surge and had to settle for second place. It's well worth noting that Iris's Gift never finished out of the first two in all his races over hurdles, so defeat here was against another exceptional talent emerging in this division.

Victory the following season in the Long Distance Hurdle at Newbury under AP McCoy for the first time, set Baracouda up for his next target, the Long Walk Hurdle, a race he had already won three times.

The Ascot race was transferred to the Berkshire riverside course of Windsor on 18 December 2004. Baracouda, now rising ten, faced seven opponents on the figure of eight circuit.

Two outsiders, Kadara and Ilnamar took the field along, the former setting up a clear lead, with the fancied Crystal D'Ainay in third. McCoy held Baracouda in mid division while the other joint second favourite, Rule Supreme, was held up at the rear.

Crystal D'Ainay moved through to lead before three out only for the famous green and gold silks to be seen stalking through after him, Rule Supreme running on but too far back by now. As they approached the last Baracouda hit the front and started to idle, but the odds on shot had too much in hand on Crystal D'Ainay and the fast finishing Rule Supreme.

In the winners enclosure he was warmly greeted, job done, the crowd unaware that in landing the Long Walk Hurdle for a record breaking fourth time, they had just witnessed Baracouda's last victory.

Back at Cheltenham, Rule Supreme confirmed the form by taking third spot in the newly named World Hurdle behind his Windsor conqueror, but the monster which was Baracouda had met another rising superstar in Inglis Drever.

In November the two met again at Newbury where Inglis Drever had to pull out all the stops to beat his four year older opponent again in a driving finish.

Inglis Drever missed the World Hurdle due to injury, yet twenty runners faced the starter for what would prove to be Baracouda's last race. Eleven years old and again on ground far from his ideal he came with a run between the last two which had his many fans hoping for a fairytale ending but time had crept up on him and the younger brigade were just too strong for the old fellow. A gallant and lovingly applauded fifth place was the only time he had not finished in the first two places since Francois Doumen took over his training six years earlier.

JP McManus, a true lover of horses as well as horseracing took Baracouda back to his Martinstown stud in County Limerick for a well earned retirement where he loped around the paddocks with his long term companion, First Gold.

The next time Big Buck's is compared to Inglis Drever or even Iris's Gift as the best of the staying hurdle division, remember where it all really took off. Perhaps the best of them all, Baracouda.

BEST MATE

The day had started out bright and sunny and relatively mild for the first day of November 2005, but it was to finish so dark and cold it was like a waking nightmare.

Exeter racecourse, high up in the Devon hills, for the Haldon Gold Cup. I took my youngest daughter, Demelza, racing with me as a treat. You see she loved Best Mate. I promised her she'd see him race and the delight on her face as we set off just to see the horse whose pictures and book adorned her bedroom was worth the early morning detour to the stable to see to her own pony, Dash.

Even before the second race of the day had finished we had found a spot on the rail of the pre-parade ring to see the horses prepare for the big race of the day.

Three or four of the best steeplechasers around, including Kauto Star and Monkerhostin, had plodded past before the star of the show himself appeared. I doubt Exeter have had many bigger crowds over the years as thousands had poured in just to see this one horse with the trestle table at the back of the grandstand doing a roaring trade in Best Mate rosettes, mugs, posters and scarves. Packed around the pre-parade ring, couples, perhaps racing for the first time, fathers showing their children, even mothers showing their babies, look, there's Best Mate.

Although he had never finished out of the first two in his whole racing life, we all knew that he wasn't really expected to win today...it didn't matter, we were all there just to *see* him and see him we did. In all his majesty he looked simply magnificent, well honed and ready to race. His beautiful head knew how good he was and in the parade ring nothing looked in the same class. Duly he won the Best Turned Out award and I set off to the betting ring to help myself to some of the 12/1 on offer, feeling that if he ran even half as good as he looked it would take a very good horse to beat him. After all he was a living legend, a triple Cheltenham Gold Cup winner, the first since Arkle and potentially every bit as good, if not better.

We set off down the course to stand at the last fence where I managed to take several good photographs for my daughters' collection, one with Best Mate looking straight at us, posing, knowing he was the centrepiece of the day, then they were off.

Best Mate was up with the action from the outset and jumping well, as he always did, giving his best in that seemingly effortless manner until he started to fall slowly behind in the back straight. In hindsight I think something may have been going amiss with him even here.

The racecourse commentary didn't mention him as the leaders raced around the turn and up the home straight. A great race was being fought out over the final few fences, but many faces were turned back down the course, looking for Best Mate. I was standing just along from Henrietta Knight with the cheers ringing out as Monkerhostin won from Kauto Star. Eventually Best Mate came cantering slowly into view, passing around the second last fence, having evidently been pulled up, then he seemed to falter badly and almost in slow motion Best Mate then just collapsed to the ground barely twenty yards away, his fantastic presence ebbing fast away.

Women and children were suddenly in floods of tears. Cries of; "don't look, don't look", echoed as more people rushed to see what had happened. The grief for a horse was awful. It was just a horse, after all. No, it wasn't, it was Best Mate, a Champion, a Legend, a gentleman of the equine world who was loved by all. Those not in tears were stunned by shock. Total strangers shared their grief with their fellows. They hugged and they cried together as their hero lay dead on the cold, damp turf.

Eventually a horse ambulance arrived and the dead body of a great horse was taken away, the dreaded green screens pulled down and only a bare patch of ground remained.

By whatever fate rules these sort of things, the very next race was won by Henrietta Knight's Racing Demon and the cheers rang out loud and long. Poor Racing Demon may have imagined the cheers were for him, but they weren't. The cheers were for Best Mate. With tears still fresh in many eyes, the crowd was cheering one last time for their hero, for the pleasure he had brought to all our lives, cheering him one last time for what he meant to us all, but Best Mate could now no longer hear the adulation which had been his by right.

The King is dead, but despite the horror of the day he will live in our memories for ever.

BRADBURY STAR

When asked what the key attributes are in a top National Hunt jockey the stock answers are skill, courage, dedication etc, etc. In this sport, unlike many others, there is one other extremely important factor which is crucial in the very best jockeys... they have to be absolutely insane. Not just potty or a bit mad, but totally crackers.

To hurl yourself over a series of birch fences at over 30mph on top of a horse, with sometimes dozens of other runners waiting to trample all over you if you fall off is crazy enough. To shrug off the many bumps, bruises and broken collar bones and carry on, knowing full well that it's going to happen again and again defies belief in us lesser mortals.

Having made that point, let's have a look at Saturday 13th November 1993 where the Mackeson Gold Cup is run at Cheltenham racecourse.

For this first classic of the jumping season quite a large field was gathered for which the 11/2 favourite, having been heavily backed ante-post, was the Gordon Richards trained General Pershing. Nicely weighted on 10 stone 11 pounds, General Pershing had warmed up for the race a couple of weeks beforehand when finishing second in a modest race behind the heavily backed favourite. His last eight runs of the previous season had netted 6 wins and 2 second places and many expected a strong showing here at Cheltenham.

Another well fancied runner was Storm Alert who had won his only race of the current season, beating the brilliant Young Snugfit in the process. With five wins from 6 races in the previous season, where his only reverse was in coming 3rd when favourite under a big weight in the Grand Annual at the Cheltenham Festival, it would be easy to see him winning here as well.

The blinkered Egypt Mill Prince was Jenny Pitman's runner. The 9/1 shot had also won his only race of the season so far, slaughtering a moderate field under a huge weight and again a big run was expected by his connections.

At 6/1, the second favourite was Second Schedule, now with David Nicholson, having recently won two hurdle races in the space of 3 days at Listowel in Ireland for Arthur Moore. He wasn't out of the frame in eight races in the '92-'93 season, which included a fine second place in Cheltenham's Tripleprint Gold Cup and winning the Cathcart at the Festival from another of the days' runners, General Idea, who, incidentally, had finished 4th in the '92 Mackeson.

Quite simply the field was oozing class, the majority of which seemed to produce their best form around Cheltenham's unique undulations.

Despite this, and the top weighted presence of former Champion Hurdler, Morley Street, in the field, one other runner carried such confidence that defeat was not an option.

In his novice season, 2 years ago, Bradbury Star carried all before him, winning seven races, including the Scilly Isles Novice Chase at Sandown and the Mumm Novice Chase at Aintree where Jodami was given 3 pounds and a ¾ length beating. Only in the Sun Alliance Chase did he succumb by a mere ½ length to Miinnehoma.

Last season he won only one race but was never out of the first four, putting up good performances in the H + T Walker Gold Cup at Ascot, the King George at Kempton and the Racing Post Chase at the same course.

Three weeks prior to today's race he made his heavily backed seasonal debut, leading at the last fence to beat Garrison Savannah and now the sights of trainer Josh Gifford, jockey Declan Murphy, owner James Campbell and many others were set for Cheltenham where victory was surely just a matter of turning up as no-one even remotely connected with the horse expected anything other than bashing the bookies where it hurts them the most.

Jockey Declan Murphy was easily one of the best jockeys of the era, possessing all of the traits of a top class jockey in spades. He was really keyed up for this race, so it was just as well that he also had a strong hand in that other crucial requirement, being a total lunatic.

Imagine then, you have a top class horse in a top class race but half an hour earlier you are riding a very dodgy jumper called Arcot in a handicap hurdle. He's going as well as a favourite should be, closing fast on the leader going to the second last when he falls and absolutely buries his jockey. Any sane person would take the rest of the day off, but not Declan; not with Bradbury Star and the Mackeson Gold Cup next up. With a thundering headache, blurred double vision and barely able to stand up he somehow passed the racecourse doctor and took the mount on Bradbury Star.

Guiburns Nephew was the early leader, Brandeston unseating his rider at the first fence until Egypt Mill Prince went on from the 3rd at a cracking pace. Storm Alert, Second Schedule, General Pershing and Bradbury Star were always prominent with Guiburns Nephew while Morley Street was well behind and never really in the race at all.

By half way Egypt Mill Prince had a clear lead and at the 10th fence General Pershing was being niggled along while Bradbury Star, having to do the best he could with his far from fit jockey made a mistake, then another at the 12th where Guiburns Nephew blundered badly and unseated Chris Maude.

Egypt Mill Prince was still galloping strongly as the field approached three from home, Second Schedule having made good progress to dispute second place, Storm Alert going well, General Pershing back on the bit with every chance and Bradbury Star confidently tracking these.

At three out Second Schedule slipped on landing, giving Adrian Maguire no chance as they fell. Storm Alert now came under strong pressure and was starting to weaken and by the next fence General Pershing was only running on at one pace.

Bradbury Star was cruising through the field on the bit, reducing Egypt Mill Prince's advantage to just two lengths by the penultimate fence, where the latter hit it hard but still had a narrow advantage at the last.

Half way up the run in Declan Murphy shook the reins at Bradbury Star, driving him clear to win emphatically by seven lengths from Egypt Mill Prince, who in turn was followed home by General Pershing and Storm Alert.

It was a brilliant victory for Bradbury Star who just a month later would fail by only a short head to win Kempton's King George in a thrilling finish with Barton Bank. In March he would start second favourite for the Cheltenham Gold Cup, finishing fifth behind The Fellow and Jodami and the following season he would win the Mackeson again, this time from Second Schedule with Egypt Mill Prince in third place.

On this day, however, a horse that simply loved Cheltenham proved his superstar status to all those who hadn't seen it clearly before. Bradbury Star won as they always knew he would and Declan Murphy, he took the rest of the afternoon off.

MORLEY STREET

It takes an exceptional race horse to win a top class race for three consecutive years, but to win a particular race four times is so rare that members of this prestigious club can be counted in single figures.

Way back in 1989 a novice hurdler began a love affair with Aintree racecourse by winning the 2 mile 4 furlong novice hurdle by one and a half lengths at odds of 7/2 from the 3/1 favourite, Trapper John. The following April Morley Street was back for Aintree's showpiece two and a half mile hurdle event. On this occasion he scored by a very easy 15 lengths from Joyful Noise as the 4/5 favourite. On to 1991 and our hero returned as the Champion Hurdler this time and starting as favourite again, at 11/8, he trounced Nomadic Way by a comfortable 6 lengths.

In 1992 Morley Street lost his hurdling crown at Cheltenham and then had to pull out all the stops at Aintree. Although 4/5 favourite he had to be ridden right out to beat the Irish mare, Minorette's Girl by a mere half a length. If this had been his farewell to Aintree he would have signed off with wins in each of the last four years, the final three in the Grade 1 Aintree Hurdle itself.

The great joy of National Hunt horses is that they turn out year after year and Morley Street returned in 1993 to attempt the near impossibility of a four timer.

The 1993 renewal looked a far stronger race and Morley Street was no longer the force he once was with only one win from five starts. The season started well for him when he met his full brother, Granville Again in the Coral Elite hurdle at Cheltenham, winning a very tactical affair by a length, giving away 6 pounds. Granville Again then reversed the form when they filled the minor roles in the Bula hurdle, beating Morley Street by 6 lengths.

In the Christmas Hurdle at Kempton, Granville Again was the 11/10 favourite but could only finish third, beaten five lengths and three by the unbeaten Mighty Mogul and Flown.

On to the Champion Hurdle itself and while Morley Street finished a very disappointing 12th at 20/1, his brother, Granville Again took the crown in fine style. Flown, who had finished ahead of him at Kempton was a very heavily backed 7/2 favourite but finished only 8th while another good horse, Ruling was far from right and pulled up at half way.

With Champion Hurdler, Granville Again, Flown and Ruling in the field, the 9 year old Morley Street would have it all to do if he were to continue his unbeaten record at Aintree. To make matters even worse for him, two very good Irish horses were contesting the prize as well.

Novello Allegro had recently finished just two and a half lengths behind Royal Derbi in the Irish Champion Hurdle...Royal Derbi then finished just 2 lengths behind Granville Again when second in the Champion Hurdle itself, so a line here would give Novello Allegro a very good chance and the Charlie Swan ridden 5 year old would start at 15/2 at Aintree. Prior to these he had finished just over 4 lengths ahead of Crowded House, the last of the days runners, when they both finished just ahead of former Champion Hurdler Royal Gait, who sadly collapsed and died just after the winning post.

As the race got under way on the firm ground which Morley Street always preferred, it was Flown, the 7/2 second favourite who set a good pace under Richard Dunwoody with Ruling and Peter Niven just ahead of the Adrian Maguire ridden Crowded House.

Novello Allegro and Peter Scudamore's champion, Granville Again, the heavily backed 10/11 favourite came next with Morley Street, this time a 6/1 shot bringing up the rear for Graham Bradley, his new partner.

Crowded House was never fluent in the first time blinkers while Ruling, who had drifted badly in the betting made several mistakes early on. At the seventh flight Flown made a mistake while Morley Street made smooth progress to take closer order. Flown made another mistake two hurdles later and Granville Again was suddenly chasing the leaders to take closer order in the fast run race.

Novello Allegro had been nicely held up but was quickly outpaced as the tempo increased and lost touch four from home where Crowded House also weakened through the field.

Three out and Flown quickened yet again on the fast ground, still trying to win from the front while Granville Again and Ruling were being hard ridden to stay in touch. In total contrast to these three, Morley Street was going with exceptional ease and the massed crowds were beginning to sense something special about to happen…they were not to be disappointed!

Flown approached the last under strong pressure from Dunwoody but the elegant chestnut head of Morley Street suddenly ranged into view, going with ominous ease, looking as if he were just cantering to the start. Together they jumped the last, Flown flat out under strong driving while Morley Street was still, incredibly, being held up, so close that his head was practically touching Dunwoody's boot.

Ruling was staying on well while Granville Again was being galvanised by Scudamore, closing down fast, wide and late.

With the crowd roaring as never before and only 50 yards left to run, Bradley then asked Morley Street and he shot past Flown while Granville Again could never get any closer.

Morley Street won by a comfortable one and a half lengths from Granville Again with 2 lengths back to Flown and another head to Ruling.

Sadly Morley Street never won another race, but he'd done enough. A Champion Hurdle, two Breeders' Cup Steeplechases in America and an incredible four Aintree Hurdles to take his place with the very best of all time, and what a way to do it, on Grand National day.

Who won the National later that afternoon? Who cares…we'd just seen Morley Street win the race of the season.

CARVILL'S HILL

It seems that every other season an untried horse is hyped up as the next world beater, the proverbial "talking horse". Invariably these beasts emanate from the emerald isle and are hailed as the new Arkle.

In virtually every case the latest super horse fails to live up to the heady expectations the connections had led the public to expect. Many is the list and many more will appear over the years with only the bare few attaining the heights the hype had alluded to.

There is, however, a possible exception to this trend in a horse that was built up and up and despite a very good race record is best remembered for the race he didn't win and the horrendous jumping mistakes he made.

Ask anyone who saw him race what their impression is of Carvill's Hill and you can guarantee the answer will be; "bad jumper, always fell over, never won much". It's true that his jumping was often a worry but he did, in fact, only fall three times in his racing life.

Born on January 1st 1982 it would be the best part of ten years before he produced his most exhilarating performance and then a bare two months before running the race which follows him around like a black cloud to this day.

As the 1986/87 season was starting to wind down, Carvill's Hill took to the racecourse for the first time, winning two 2 mile National Hunt flat races, the latter under the steadier of 12 stone 5 pounds.

The following season he took to hurdles and was a short priced favourite each time, three of them at odds on, winning 4 of his five races and finishing second in the other one. The talk was beginning and Carvill's Hill was now the latest in a long line of horses where the expectations were growing far faster than his blossoming talent.

December 17th 1988 saw his fencing debut over 2 miles at Navan and he started at odds on again in a field of 10 but won with ease. After that he was sent to Leopardstown on Boxing day and a horrendous mistake sent him crashing with the race at his mercy.

Stepped up to 2½ miles he then put a distance between himself and his pursuers and followed this with an emphatic win at his first attempt over three miles, but each time there was the spectre of him meeting the odd fence totally wrong.

Next up for this big, strong horse with the raking stride was the Cheltenham Gold Cup for which he started at 5/1 behind Desert Orchid. The hope of Ireland was again let down by his jumping and crashed out of the race and then galloped free with an earlier faller, Golden Freeze. This pair would be the subject of major controversy in the race 3 years later. As it was, Carvill's Hill returned to Ireland and easily won both of his remaining races that season.

Over the next couple of seasons he ran only six times due to injuries, never leaving Irish shores. His jumping was unfortunately as erratic as ever, yet he was still lauded wherever and whenever he ran.

At Punchestown he found the useful Maid of Money 3 lengths too good before trouncing First Noel by 15 lengths and then Barney Burnett by an easy 6 lengths in his next two races although every time punters were far more worried by his jumping than by the opposition. His last race that season was the Irish Hennessy Cognac Gold Cup at Leopardstown where, despite being an odds on favourite again, he couldn't match the fluid jumping of the English raider, Nick the Brief, who was virtually unbeatable in this race over the years. Indeed some felt that Carvill's Hill did especially well just to stay upright as he met more than one fence totally wrong.

Eight months later and a new season saw him resume winning ways before another crashing fall ended his season at Gowran Park.

By now Carvill's Hill was being classified as yet another under-achiever whose jumping was so suspect you daren't back him and then an event occurred which ensured Carvill's Hill will always be remembered. Millionaire owner Paul Green bought him and eventually transferred the big horse to the all-conquering Martin Pipe yard.

As a ten year old and ridden by Peter Scudamore for the first time, a not yet racing fit Carvill's Hill dished out a 10 length beating to Aquilifer and was resoundingly back in business.

On 21st December 1991 Chepstow racecourse ran the 3¾ mile Welsh Grand National for which Carvill's Hill was made the 9/4 favourite despite the steadier of 11 stone 12 pounds. This race was, without doubt, his finest hour. It may be a cliché to say a horse galloped the opposition into submission but that is exactly what this magnificent beast did at Chepstow. Carvill's Hill jumped superbly, never putting a hoof wrong and simply galloped away from the opposition to win as he pleased by 20 lengths from Party Politics, who was receiving a stone and five pounds from the winner.

Suddenly Carvill's Hill was back. A new stable and a new jockey and his jumping had miraculously come together and his fitness ensured he had become the world beater everyone had been saying he was for so many years ... all he had to do now was to win the Cheltenham Gold Cup for which he was to start the even money favourite after another effortless win in his warm up race. In truth Martin Pipe had worked very long and hard to remedy a quite serious back injury when he first arrived from Ireland and an awful lot of swimming and patience had brought him to fitness while taking him back to the basics of long-reining over poles and small jumps had brought about the improvement in his jumping. Now for the pinnacle of National Hunt racing.

The bald facts of the 1992 Cheltenham Gold Cup will show that Toby Balding's Cool Ground won by a short head from The Fellow. What they don't show is that in a properly run race Carvill's Hill would very probably have won, but didn't due entirely to the tactics Jenny Pitman gave her jockey aboard Golden Freeze.

Golden Freeze was a very good, if not Gold Cup class, horse in his own right and Mrs Pitman decided that the only way that Carvill's Hill could be beaten was by getting him to fall. Thus, despite not being against the rules of racing, she decided on spoiling tactics. Every time Carvill's Hill quickened, Golden Freeze would quicken that bit more and every time Carvill's Hill eased up, Golden Freeze did the same. In this way Golden Freeze was normally about half a length ahead of Carvill's Hill in the anticipation that when Golden Freeze jumped it would get

Carvill's Hill to jump too soon and fall. Although legitimate tactics it was morally reprehensible and Mrs Pitman was widely criticised for ruining the race. As a result poor old Carvill's Hill was never able to run his race and trailed in a distant fifth of the eight runners. Despite these obvious spoiling tactics a horrendous jump at the first and then ballooning the second fence had brought about a recurrence of Carvill's Hill's back injury and he showed incredible bravery to still be in contention until the home turn. Martin Pipe was aware early in the race that his superstar could not win even before the attentions of Golden Freeze. It is to Martin Pipe's credit that he accepted the situation, although he did state much later; "Reflecting on the team tactics used to defeat us, I have only one observation to make: how much fuss would Jenny Pitman have caused had the roles been reversed?"

So, was Carvill's Hill an over hyped, bad jumping horse who never achieved his true potential?

Sadly he didn't win the Cheltenham Gold Cup he should have done but he did win 17 of his 24 races and was second in three others. Despite some horrific blunders, only on three occasions did he actually fall. Without the 1992 Gold Cup his form figures read: 11121111F11F1121121F111

Fifth in the Cheltenham Gold Cup to spoiling tactics in what proved to be his last ever race is the only blot on an otherwise impeccable record.

To those who remember Carvill's Hill as a bad jumper and a "nearly" horse, remember that December day at Chepstow when a big, gallant horse turned the Welsh Grand National into a virtual procession with an exquisite display of galloping and jumping. Remember Carvill's Hill as a champion who all but fulfilled the heady expectations that followed him since his early days. If he had won the Gold Cup which had his name on it he would be lauded still, so don't let one race tarnish the memory of a great horse, Carvill's Hill.

ELSICH

Only in England could the racehorse Quixall Crossett not only have been well known, but actually have had his own fan club.

Quixall Crossett could not accurately be described as a racehorse, yet appear in races against other horses is what he did. He was loved by his owners and the racing public who knew full well that he hadn't a hope in hell of ever winning a race but however slow he ran he always gave it his best shot. In all, Quixall Crossett ran in 103 races and although he never managed to win, twice he finished second and filled the third place on no less than six occasions to amass £8,502 in prize money throughout his career. It is interesting to note that in 55 of those races he beat at least one horse home, of which twice he finished ahead of 8 other rivals and ahead of 7 on three other occasions.

To many minds this admirable beast wears the crown as the worst horse to ever set hoof on a racecourse. It may come as a surprise, then, to learn that a horse which actually contested 3 Cheltenham Gold Cups and a Grand National would make Quixall Crossett seem like Arkle in comparison.

Back in the days of yore, a Shropshire farmer by the name of Charles E. Edwards owned a brown gelding by the name of Elsich. Foaled in 1936, this poor animal spent the first years of his life as a work horse around the farm and even pulled a holiday caravan for two weeks one summer.

In 1945, with the war still on and jump racing only taking place at Cheltenham, Windsor, Wetherby and Catterick, Edwards decided that as well as being a farmer he was also a racehorse trainer and the 9 year old Elsich was actually a racehorse.

And so it was that on February 17, having secured the services of a jockey by the name of Silvester, Elsich lined up at Cheltenham for the

Charlton Kings Chase over 2 miles. In hindsight, calling Edwards a trainer was a shade short of the mark as Elsich had no idea what was about to happen as he galloped headlong into the first fence, when perhaps over it may have been a better option.

Somewhat miffed that his stable star had fluffed his debut, Edwards declared him for the Cirencester Chase to be run over 3 miles an hour and a half later. It came as no surprise that Silvester ran a mile when asked to renew the partnership and a new jockey had to be found in the shape of one Redmond who steered Elsich as far as the fifth fence before they parted company.

At the next Cheltenham meeting Redmond had retained the ride but decided to pull Elsich up when they were over two fences behind the rest of the field.

With no Grand National to be run again that year and the Cheltenham Gold Cup renewed after a two year break, this would be the first major steeplechase for nearly three years, run as a one day meeting on Saturday 17 March.

Despite form figures of "FFP", Edwards had no hesitation in declaring Elsich for the race which attracted a record entry of 16 runners on a clear, bright day with perfect going.

At the business end of the race the front three in the betting had the race to themselves with Schubert and Paladin together over the last before Red Rower powered through on the final hill to win for his Owner/Trainer/Breeder, Lord Stalbridge as the 11/4 favourite. For the record Elsich refused at the fifth.

His last race of the season was again at Cheltenham where Elsich fell at the second fence but Edwards was clearly not perturbed by this initial lack of success and Elsich duly appeared again the following season.

Having failed to complete the course in his five runs so far, Elsich extended that sequence with a further 5 falls, 1 "refused", 1 "pulled up" and a race at Cheltenham where he apparently unseated his rider on the flat. Popular opinion has it that the jockey actually threw himself off in panic.

Elsich turned out again 24 hours later where, for the very first time in 14 races he finished a race, albeit a quarter of a mile behind the winner.

Perhaps things had finally clicked for Elsich as the next time he ran he collected the princely sum of £20 in prize money when finishing third at Worcester. In truth it was only a three horse race and he was already a long way tailed off last when he slowly clambered over the final obstacle, but it was a start.

Back at Cheltenham again for his next two races the form book reads, "00" against his name although a little scrutiny reveals that Elsich actually fell in both races and was bravely remounted each time.

His next entry, on 14 March, was another crack at the Cheltenham Gold Cup for which he would start at 200/1 in a field of six.

An eleven year old Irish super horse with an enormous reputation called Prince Regent started as the 4/7 favourite where only Poor Flame and Red April were considered to have any chance against him.

To his eternal credit it was none other than the gallant Elsich under W. Balfe that led the Gold Cup field from the second to the 5th fence. Unfortunately he soon weakened in this class and while Prince Regent slipped and all but fell on the top bend before powering home to glory, Elsich, in splendid isolation, contrived to fall at the water jump second time around.

As you would expect now of Edwards, the next logical race had to be the Grand National where Edwards invested £10 at the mean spirited odds of only 25/1 about Elsich getting round the Aintree fences. It is amazing to recount that Edwards slept in the adjoining box on the night before the race as he feared a potential doping plot against his horse! In the race itself Lovely Cottage now appears in the history pages as the winner while Elsich predictably fell at the first.

After Aintree, Elsich recorded the sort of form figures which, to the uninitiated, may look like he was finally producing the goods which Edwards so firmly believed in as Elsich rattled up an astounding looking "2343". Again the hard truth is that Elsich was beaten in a match at Ludlow at odds of 33/1, the shortest odds at which he was ever to start. He followed this on the same course with a distant third of 3, went to Woore to finish tailed off fourth of 4 and then on to Towcester to take third spot in another three horse race, again a very long way behind the other finishers.

In the 1946 - '47 season Elsich notched up no less than 27 appearances, more than any other horse in training that year, opening his account with a long way last of 6 at Ludlow before normal activities were resumed.

Elsich failed to complete the course in ten of his next 13 races, of which one of the "duck eggs" was achieved at Leicester when his jockey, Tommy Cross, bravely remounted at both the penultimate and last fences.

On April 7 at Hereford a new jockey was found in Renfield Jenkins who would partner Elsich for the rest of the season, falling only once in 14 races, an astounding transformation in itself! On their first start together Elsich was a tailed off last of four but his day of glory was not far away now.

April 12 was Cheltenham Gold Cup day where Lord Grimthorpe's 6 year old Fortina scored a 10 length victory over Dorothy Paget's 3/1 favourite Happy Home. Elsich, at only 100/1 this year, hit the second fence so hard it is amazing that Jenkins stayed in the plate at all, but less surprising that he pulled up before attempting the next obstacle.

And so on to Elsich's date with destiny, recorded forever in posterity as 24 April 1947 at Woore racecourse. To his eternal credit, Renfield Jenkins galvanised Elsich on this day and the pair set off in front and made the running to half way before succumbing and even then staying on well to finish a gallant 16 lengths 3rd of six to Desert Lover. After all this time Elsich had at long last not only finished in front of another horse, he had beaten three of them at once!

At Newport on June 14 Elsich ran what was to be his last race, and refused.

In October 1947, still undeterred, Edwards made his first entry of the new season for Elsich. The Stewards of the National Hunt Committee returned the entry fee and curtly informed Edwards that no more entries for the horse would ever be accepted...Elsich's racing days were finally over.

Two things stand out in this tale ahead of any others. Not what a rotten trainer Edwards was, or how poor a beast Elsich must have been but what an exceptionally resilient horse he must have been to stand the rigours he was put through and what a brave, or stupid, horse he was not to have refused more often than he did.

So the next time someone cites Quixall Crossett or some other beast as the worst racehorse of all time, you now know better. Equally, if you happen to own a racehorse of dubious merits remember Elsich at Woore in 1947, as, at least to some degree, every dog has its day.

WHO IS THE GREATEST?

Kauto Star and Denman discuss the question.
Photograph by Graham Buddry.

The first Saturday of January 2010 saw turf racing frozen off again and while Channel 4 racing brought the best of the very poor offerings from the All Weather tracks, it was their in-depth discussions which made compulsive viewing.

With the aid of Ted Walsh, the team tried to answer the perennial question; Who is the Greatest. Needless to say it was a lively and ultimately futile discussion for two simple reasons. Firstly, never let facts get in the way and only quote those which support your own opinion while conveniently ignoring all other facts.

The second and far more important reason why the question can never be settled is down to unsurpassable personal bias. Ted Walsh, for instance, while extremely knowledgeable can never see past an Irish trained winner of every race at the Cheltenham Festival, thus making his analysis on Channel 4 extremely prejudiced. It comes as no surprise, then, when Walsh emphatically states that Arkle is the best of all time and throws in only the facts that support his viewpoint. In exactly the same way you will never find any Irishman that doesn't firmly believe that Arkle will always remain at the pinnacle. Don't get me wrong, Arkle was awesome, but if you can't see past National pride or an anti-everything-English viewpoint then trying to answer the age old question is impossible.

Here I'm going to take an unbiased look at all the facts, arguments and counter-arguments and hopefully attempt to answer the question, knowing full well that the majority of people will shake their heads and disagree whatever the outcome.

The three obvious contenders are Golden Miller, Arkle and Kauto Star but I'll be adding a few others into the mix, not just for the fun of it but because they deserve to be included.

The first, and perhaps most famous, fact to look at is the one all advocates of Arkle routinely trot out...When Arkle was in a race there had to be two handicaps drawn up, one if he raced and another if he was scratched. If this was to be the true definitive of greatness then Arkle would be firmly in *second* place!

Most race fans know that the first Grand National was won by Lottery, but how many know that Lottery was even more superior to his contempories than Arkle was. Arkle may have had the unique distinction of having two handicaps drawn up when he was due to run but in the late 1830's and early 1840's race conditions regularly stated; "Open to all horses except Lottery".

This brings me neatly to the bias factor. It is a human trait that firm allegiance is made to the first "great" we encounter, no matter what the sport. From my own perspective I firmly believe (through my own early bias) that Brigadier Gerard is the best ever seen on the flat, Comedy of Errors is the greatest hurdler of them all while Pendil and Captain Christy are inseparable in the chasing division. To prove the warped view which bias brings, in athletics I won't hear of a greater sprinter than the Russian Olympic Champion Valery Borzov, yet in truth he wouldn't get within 10 yards of Usain Bolt. In the same manner, those who saw Lottery run would never believe that any horse could ever be better.

Many, many years ago I paid a visit to the retired Desert Orchid at the house and stables of his part owner, James Burridge. Towards the end of the afternoon I asked James who he considered to be the best between Golden Miller and Arkle. With no hesitation James emphatically declared Golden Miller to be far superior. He may or may not be, but the point is that James Burridge had seen Golden Miller run in his younger days and that bias would stay with him forever. I would seriously doubt whether many who saw both these great horses run would side with Arkle due to the bias factor, anymore than those whose earliest recollections are of Arkle would see further than Himself.

Supporters of Golden Miller play their chosen fact of his incredible five victories in the Cheltenham Gold Cup and only just beaten the following year. On the bare face of it this would clearly make Golden Miller the best of all except for other certain facts. The race had not been devised in the days when Lottery was running and who can say he would not have won a similar number? More importantly though, the Gold Cup was still a new race which didn't have the status it holds today. The Grand National was by far the most important race of the year and even at Cheltenham the National Hunt Chase was more prestigious and carried more prize money. Take nothing away from Golden Miller, he could do no more than win his races and even added a Grand National to his roll of honour as well, but the Gold Cup was a different race back then.

Winning a top race for years on end brings us to Kauto Star and his three victories in the Betfair Chase, a level weights affair run at Haydock. Hang on a minute though … this race was known for many years as the Edward Hanmer Chase and Silver Buck won it four times! What's more it used to be a handicap so when Silver Buck won he was giving lumps of weight away to the likes of Burrough Hill Lad and Night Nurse, carting welter burdens to victory.

This brings us back to weight, that proverbial monster which apparently can stop trains.

Arkle again is the most famous of all in this area with his half length defeat when giving 35lbs to Stalbridge Colonist in the 1966 Hennessy Gold Cup, a horse who would finish second in the Cheltenham Gold Cup four months later. In comparison Silver Buck went down by a length when giving 34lbs to Sunset Cristo, a horse who would finish 12 lengths back in 3rd place behind Silver Buck in the 1982 Cheltenham Gold Cup. A little known co-incidence here is that Arkle and Silver Buck are actually related. Arkle's sire, Archive, was also the sire of Silver Buck's dam, Choice Archlesse.

Superb weight carrying performance can be attributed to almost all of the main contenders where perhaps Lottery leads the way. Having won the first Grand National in 1839, he was allotted an incredible 13st 4lbs for the 1840 renewal. Golden Miller, Arkle, Silver Buck and Desert Orchid regularly humped burdens of 12 stone or more in handicaps, winning far more than they ever lost. Kauto Star is the exception yet it is not really of his making. In this modern era weights are limited to 11.10 and with so many good races around there is no real need for Kauto Star to be aimed at handicaps in the way his predecessors were.

With modern training methods, too, there is no need to "get a run into him" in the ways where only a race or two could truly get a horse fit. There is nothing better than seeing the real superstars competing regularly throughout a season but whereas Golden Miller, Arkle, Silver Buck and Desert Orchid would compete many times each year, the likes of Kauto Star, Denman, Best Mate and triple Champion Hurdler, See You Then (cruelly nicknamed "See You When") average only three appearances each season, making it hard to build the wonderful affinity which these champions deserve.

The next fact to look at is winning times and again the Arkle camp are quick off the mark to cite his Gallagher Gold Cup victory at Sandown over three miles as a mark which still stands today. To my mind it was undoubtedly Arkle's best run and a seeming benchmark on which to make comparisons. Unfortunately it isn't as easy as that. If record times were the definitive answer to the question Golden Miller would usurp Arkle. In the 1934 Grand National, a course he simply loathed, Golden Miller lugged 12.2 to victory in a course record time which stood until Red Rum bettered it when carrying only 10.5 in his titanic battle with Crisp almost 40 years later.

If record winning times were the answer we would be including the likes of Tingle Creek to the equation for his multiple record time performances around Sandown and excluding Silver Buck who only did as much as he had to, so we have to look deeper.

Those who saw Kauto Star obliterate his field in the King George on Boxing day 2009 saw one of the greatest ever performances and to be there among the packed throngs was a privilege but you have to ask yourself, what did he actually beat? Take nothing away from Kauto Star, it was a fantastic effort but in the cold light of day he didn't beat anything of note. If you compare that to Desert Orchid whose fields included Cheltenham Gold Cup winners Forgive 'n' Forget, Burrough Hill Lad and The Fellow as well as the brilliant Wayward Lad, Kauto Star had it easy.

On the strength of the opposition there were a lot more top class chasers around in the '70s and '80s especially, therefore the races took more winning. Compare the 1982 Cheltenham Gold Cup victory of Silver Buck in a record field of 22 runners where the quality included Bregawn, Tied Cottage, Master Smudge, Night Nurse and Diamond Edge among others to Arkle's three victories against just 3 others in 1964, which included a 20/1 and 50/1 shot, 3 others again in 1965 where two were priced at 33/1 and 100/1 and 4 other runners in 1966 which again included 33/1 and 50/1 outsiders. Without sounding too unkind, even a donkey race has to have a victor and if that donkey is far superior to the opposition, he too will appear to be a world beater. On the plus side, Arkle could only beat what was in front of him and he did it with ease.

Victories in the Cheltenham Gold Cup, once it was firmly established, would leave Arkle and Kauto Star well ahead of Silver Buck and Desert

Orchid while King George wins would leave Arkle languishing behind so perhaps we should look at the "what if" factor.

Desert Orchid hated Cheltenham to such an extent that he ran stones worse there than anywhere else. What if the Gold Cup had been run elsewhere? Desert Orchid would probably have won more than once, but this is stretching the bounds too far for our task in hand. Desert Orchid should, however, have five wins in the King George to his name as the break in the sequence was a second place to Nupsala. You would be hard pressed to find anyone who believes Nupsala was a better horse than Desert Orchid around Kempton and he won purely because Desert Orchid lost. In this I mean that Desert Orchid could not win due to the suicidal early pace where he and Beau Ranger covered the first half mile faster than the runners in that years 2000 Guineas had at Newmarket when carrying 3 stone less! With a sensible early pace I can't see how Desert Orchid could possibly have lost.

Moving on to Silver Buck with a Gold Cup and two King George's to his name. After two emphatic victories at Kempton, Silver Buck was primed for a hat-trick when fate intervened. The meeting was lost to the weather and Silver Buck actually turned out lame a day before. Again I have no doubt that fit and at the top of his game, had the race been run he would have sauntered home as he had the previous two years. The following year Silver Buck jumped the last upsides Wayward Lad and Fifty Dollars More before being run out of it in the closing stages. The following day a severe throat infection was diagnosed and a long trip to a vetinary unit in Bristol for a minor operation ensued. Using the "what if" factor, Silver Buck would have four victories in the King George to his name.

In 1980, Silver Buck was a late withdrawal from the Cheltenham Gold Cup due to the ground, even though jockey Tommy Carmody thought it wouldn't be a problem. The subsequently disqualified Tied Cottage beat Master Smudge on ground which Silver Buck won on later in his career. In the same manner that neither of those two were in the same league as Silver Buck, the "what if" factor dictates that if he had run he would have won. The following year Silver Buck was cantering all over Night Nurse and Little Owl as these three drew away from the rest on the run down the hill for the final time. It was clear there would only be one winner yet Silver Buck stopped as if shot two out, finishing third. All of Michael Dickinson's runners, including Badsworth Boy and Wayward Lad, severely under performed that week and a stable virus was later diagnosed. To put this into a true perspective, in all the times Silver Buck and Night Nurse faced each other, this was the only occasion when Night Nurse came out in front. Using the "what if" factor, this then gives Silver Buck three Cheltenham Gold Cups.

Arkle already has a fine record but the "what if" factor applies perhaps more to him than any of the others. It is a sad fact that his racing career was brought to an end when he fractured a pedal bone at Kempton, yet bravely still finished second that day. Without that untimely accident it is hard to see how he would have been beaten there or in the Gold Cup three months later. In all probability Arkle would have added a third King George and a fifth Gold Cup to his C.V. before age took its inevitable toll on his exceptional abilities.

Golden Miller was incredibly sound and his numerous victories at Hurst Park could perhaps be viewed as a marker in place of the King George which had not then been thought up in his day. Lottery is harder to assess as very few reliable records exist, suffice to say that he would have been very hard to beat no matter what races he contested.

In the heady days of Michael Dickinson's dominance of the game he was once asked how his crop of stars and other chasers of the day would compare to the likes of Golden Miller and Easter Hero, to which Dickinson replied; "The old timers wouldn't have a cat in hell's chance. Jump racing is far more competitive now than in the years before and immediately following the war. Prize money has increased and there are more runners than there used to be. Today's steeplechasers are so much faster. You only have to look at those old-time chasers to see they would have no chance against today's horses. They were like bloody great boats!"

The final fact to look at in this analysis is the ratings given by the official handicapper.

Kauto Star's brilliant performance on Boxing day 2009 raised him into fourth place on the all-time list, four pounds ahead of Desert Orchid, yet still some way behind Arkle. If you took their figures literally then Arkle is still clearly the best of all time and will probably stay that way forever but I firmly believe the ratings to be flawed!

There is no dispute from these quarters that Arkle was brilliant, a megastar of his generation and was, without question, the best we had seen. What concerns me is that Flyingbolt is rated second and Mill House third. Again I don't doubt that they were brilliant animals, but what are the chances that the three greatest horses of all time should come along at exactly the same time?

It seems obvious to these eyes that Arkle's brilliance was bestowed on Flyingbolt and Mill House simply through these ratings. As a two-miler Flyingbolt was fantastic, but should he be rated so much better than Badsworth Boy, Remittance Man, Moscow Flyer or Master Minded over the same distance. In the same vein is Mill House truly far superior to Captain Christy, Pendil, Best Mate and Denman. Take Arkle out of the equation and the answer is a clear "no".

For incredible soundness throughout a long career you cannot fault Golden Miller. For versatility over different distances Desert Orchid lands just ahead of Kauto Star, while for weight carrying achievements Arkle edges out Desert Orchid. In the manner ascribed to that progress and better facilities mean a superior athlete, Kauto Star easily leads the way.

And so, taking all of the facts, adding a big dose of "what if", looking at all performances regardless of course preference and clearing out all bias and prejudice, who really is the greatest of them all?

In truth it doesn't really matter. Let's just be thankful for having had these wonderful animals around.

Just for the record, though, I'd side with Silver Buck ... or am I being biased?

THE UK'S NO 1 HORSE RACING MONTHLY

Racing Ahead magazine is published by Racing Ahead Ltd

Contact us by:

POST: Racing Ahead Magazine, Office 113, Imperial Court, Exchange Street East, Liverpool, L3 2AB
EMAIL: info@racingahead.net
PHONE/FAX: 0845 638 0704

RACING AHEAD SUBSCRIPTIONS MAKE THE PERFECT GIFT
For just £30, you get 12 issues and, with full colour pages packed with tips, horses to follow, interviews and features, it's great value too!

You can also phone Graham Wright on 0845 638 0704 who can take your orders and payment and answer any queries you have.

Visit: www.racingahead.net